INTEGRATING LITERACY AND TECHNOLOGY

TOOLS FOR TEACHING LITERACY

Donna Ogle and Camille Blachowicz, *Series Editors*

This highly practical series includes two kinds of books: (1) grade-specific titles for first-time teachers or those teaching a particular grade for the first time; (2) books on key literacy topics that cut across all grades, such as integrated instruction, English language learning, and comprehension. Written by outstanding educators who know what works based on extensive classroom experience, each research-based volume features hands-on activities, reproducibles, and best practices for promoting student achievement. These books are suitable as texts for undergraduate- or graduate-level courses; preservice teachers will find them informative and accessible.

TEACHING LITERACY IN SIXTH GRADE
Karen Wood and Maryann Mraz

TEACHING LITERACY IN KINDERGARTEN
Lea M. McGee and Lesley Mandel Morrow

INTEGRATING INSTRUCTION: LITERACY AND SCIENCE
Judy McKee and Donna Ogle

TEACHING LITERACY IN SECOND GRADE
Jeanne R. Paratore and Rachel L. McCormack

TEACHING LITERACY IN FIRST GRADE
Diane Lapp, James Flood, Kelly Moore, and Maria Nichols

PARTNERING FOR FLUENCY
Mary Kay Moskal and Camille Blachowicz

TEACHING LITERACY THROUGH THE ARTS
Nan L. McDonald and Douglas Fisher

TEACHING LITERACY IN FIFTH GRADE
Susan I. McMahon and Jacqueline Wells

TEACHING LITERACY IN THIRD GRADE
Janice F. Almasi, Keli Garas-York, and Leigh-Ann Hildreth

INTEGRATING LITERACY AND TECHNOLOGY: EFFECTIVE PRACTICE FOR GRADES K–6
Susan Watts Taffe and Carolyn B. Gwinn

INTEGRATING LITERACY AND TECHNOLOGY

EFFECTIVE PRACTICE FOR GRADES K–6

Susan Watts Taffe
Carolyn B. Gwinn

Series Editors' Note by Donna Ogle and Camille Blachowicz

THE GUILFORD PRESS
New York   London

© 2007 The Guilford Press
A Division of Guilford Publications, Inc.
72 Spring Street, New York, NY 10012
www.guilford.com

Printed in the United States of America

This book is printed on acid-free paper.

Last digit is print number: 9 8 7 6 5 4 3 2 1

Library of Congress Cataloging-in-Publication Data

Watts-Taffe, Susan M.
  Integrating literacy and technology : effective practice for grades K–6 / by Susan Watts Taffe, Carolyn B. Gwinn.
    p. cm.—(Tools for teaching literacy)
  Includes bibliographical references and index.
  ISBN-13: 978-1-59385-452-2 ISBN-10: 1-59385-452-8 (pbk.)
  ISBN-13: 978-1-59385-453-9 ISBN-10: 1-59385-453-6 (hardcover)
  1. Educational technology—United States. 2. Technological literacy—Study and teaching. 3. Education, Elementary—United States. I. Gwinn, Carolyn B. II. Title.
  LB1028.3.W385 2007
  371.33—dc22

                                                   2006031205

To Dennis, Jonathan, and David
with love and gratitude
—S. W. T.

With a thankful heart
to Kevin, my beloved and friend; Jonathan, my special blessing;
Keith, Gordon, and Mary,
for your encouragement throughout this endeavor

In loving memory of my mother, Margaret,
who eagerly began this journey with me
and is forever in my heart
—C. B. G.

ABOUT THE AUTHORS

Susan Watts Taffe, PhD, is a researcher and consultant in the field of literacy education. In addition to literacy–technology integration, her research interests include vocabulary development, students experiencing difficulty with reading, and teacher professional development, particularly in culturally and linguistically diverse settings. A frequent speaker at state and national conferences, Dr. Watts Taffe has had articles appear in journals such as *The Reading Teacher, Language Arts, Journal of Literacy Research,* and *Reading Research Quarterly.* She has been a special education teacher and reading diagnostician. Dr. Watts Taffe spent 13 years on the faculty of the University of Minnesota, where she was associate professor of elementary and literacy education. In 1996, she received the College of Education and Human Development Distinguished Teaching Award for her work with preservice and inservice teachers. She currently resides in Cincinnati, Ohio.

Carolyn B. Gwinn, PhD, is a researcher and consultant in the field of literacy education; in this capacity, she focuses on the meaningful integration of technology into literacy curricula, infusion of best practices into literacy instruction, and the design and delivery of high-quality professional development. As an elementary curriculum specialist for one of the largest school districts in Minnesota, Dr. Gwinn engages in strategic planning, implementation, and evaluation of literacy-related initiatives and provides leadership to the district's technology and media study committee. She has presented at numerous regional and national conferences and has published articles in professional journals including *The Reading Teacher.* Dr. Gwinn has been a classroom teacher in grades 1, 4, and 5; a reading specialist; and a resource teacher. She has also taught undergraduate and graduate literacy methods courses at the University of Minnesota, where she has been recognized for her outstanding teaching and leadership in the community.

SERIES EDITORS' NOTE

This is an exciting time to be involved in literacy education. Across the United States, thoughtful practitioners and teacher educators are developing and fine-tuning their instructional practices to maximize learning opportunities for children. These cutting-edge practices deserve to be shared more broadly. Because of these changes, we have become aware of the need for a series of books for thoughtful practitioners who want a practical, research-based overview of current topics in literacy instruction. We also collaborate with staff developers and study group directors who want effective inservice materials that they can use with professionals and colleagues at many different levels that provide specific insights about literacy instruction. Thus the Tools for Teaching Literacy series was created.

This series is distinguished by having each volume written by outstanding educators who are noted for their knowledge and contributions to research, theory, and best practices in literacy education. They are also well-known staff developers who spend time in real classrooms working alongside teachers applying these insights. We think the series authors are unparalleled in these qualifications.

In this volume, Susan Watts Taffe and Carolyn B. Gwinn build on fundamental research and best practices in literacy to describe the ways in which teachers can utilize technology effectively in the literacy classroom. The volume is differentiated for teachers with varying levels of expertise and uses descriptive vignettes from real classrooms at both primary and intermediate grade levels to illustrate themes, concepts, and practical ideas.

The authors carefully guide the reader through the four major phases of instruction: planning, teaching, assessment, and reflection, illustrating the impact of technology at each phase as well as the changing role of the teacher in a technology-enriched literacy environment. They discuss various approaches to instruction such as explicit instruction, teacher modeling, think-aloud, and interactive demonstration within the context of new technologies and new literacies.

We believe this book will be an important tool for teachers as they engage students in literacies for the 21st century.

DONNA OGLE
CAMILLE BLACHOWICZ

PREFACE

tech•no•phile (n)
Somebody who is comfortable with and adapts readily to new technology or computerization.

tech•no•phobe (n)
Somebody who is intimidated and confused by new technology and computerization.

—*Encarta World English Dictionary* (1999)

tech•no•sage (n)
Somebody who is interested in making optimal use of technology for improving teaching and learning.

—THOMAS AND KING (2006)

Recently, we attended a presentation in which the speakers, Matt Thomas and Andrew King, discussed varying dispositions toward technology. A *technophile,* they explained, is someone who tends to gravitate quickly toward the new, leaving the old behind and viewing new technology as a panacea. They believe that decisions to flood schools with computers and other new technology, preceding discussions about how this technology will be used, reflect a technophile mindset. On the other end of the continuum lies the *technophobe*, who is suspicious and fearful of new technology. Assuming that there is no value in new technology, a technophobe clings to the familiar and finds comfort in the way it's always been done. Fortunately, Thomas and King suggest a middle ground between these two extremes. They define a *technosage* as someone who views technology as a promising tool, rather than an end in itself; a technosage selects technology carefully, based on the characteristics of a particular learning situation. Naturally, we like to think of ourselves as technosages, and we trust that you will soon think of yourself this way as well, if you don't already. We passionately believe that schooling must equip children with the skills and strategies they need to use technology responsibly, wisely, and effectively throughout their lives. In order to accomplish this goal, teachers must embed these skills and strategies in their instruction beginning in the elementary grades.

At its core, this book is about teacher learning in an era of rapid change and extraordinary innovation. Recognizing that educators will bring to this book a variety of beliefs, experiences, and classroom realities related to the role of new technologies in elementary school classrooms, we intend for this book to be widely relevant and accessible. Furthermore, since technology is changing rapidly, we provide many examples of technology-infused instruction that focus not only on what effective teachers are doing with technology, but on *why* they are doing what they do. We have attempted to uncover the decision making behind the instructional innovations because it is the decision making that will endure, even as the specifics of new technology continue to evolve.

We wrote this book with five goals in mind. We continually sought to:

1. Meet you wherever you are on your own literacy–technology integration journey.
2. Describe in detail the decision making behind meaningful, purpose-driven literacy–technology integration.
3. Actively engage you in processes of inquiry and reflection related to the ideas we present and your experiences with literacy–technology integration.
4. Provide hands-on strategies that you can use to propel your literacy–technology journey forward, regardless of your current teaching setting.
5. Make a sustainable impact on the ways in which you integrate technology into your instruction.

This book is designed to support you if you are reading it on your own or with others. We think the book works best when it is read by two or more teachers at once because of the power of community in learning and professional development endeavors. Some ways in which the book can be used in communities of learning are:

➢ As reading material for a teacher study group.
➢ As reading material for an instructional methods class taught in a university setting.
➢ As resource material shared between instructional coaches or teacher mentors and other teachers.
➢ As resource material for those who coordinate teacher professional development in schools and school districts.

We trust this book will be useful to you as a classroom teacher, teacher educator, professional development facilitator, or school administrator. You all play critical roles in determining the course of new technology in the lives of children and must work together to ensure that new technology is integrated into classrooms responsibly, wisely, and effectively. The resources are vast, the possibilities are great, and the time is now. Welcome to the journey of integrating literacy and technology!

ACKNOWLEDGMENTS

Many people have contributed to this book, each in a unique way. First, and foremost, we thank the teachers with whom we have worked over the past several years, especially those who are featured prominently in the pages of this volume: Jon David, Darin, Laura, Leia, Jinna, and Gail. Each of these teachers gave generously of his or her time and expertise as a member of our community of learners.

We also thank the preservice teachers enrolled in our literacy methods courses, whose passion for becoming effective teachers of reading and writing energized, inspired, and challenged us to prepare them in the best ways we knew how. Our own journey to integrate technology into our work with teachers was fueled in large part by federal funding from a PT3 (Preparing Tomorrow's Teachers for Technology) grant secured by the College of Education and Human Development at the University of Minnesota and administered by our colleague and friend Sara Dexter, whose vision was instrumental in getting us on the correct path. In our first year of work, Marcia Horn was an invaluable colleague and guide, sharing with us her knowledge and experience with technology integration. Aaron Doering, Brad Cohen, and Patricia Kubow also provided ideas and support that proved instrumental to our learning. As we continued our work, Julie Johnson and Karen Jorgensen assisted us in much of the research that provides the foundation for this book. In addition, Cathy Zemke and Karen Anderson gave us invaluable clerical support. Our efforts were further supported by our colleagues in the Department of Curriculum and Instruction; we are especially grateful to Deborah Dillon and Fred Finley.

During the process of putting our words down on paper and bringing this book to print, we appreciated the insights offered by Chris Jennison and Craig

Thomas at The Guilford Press, as well as Donna Ogle and Camille Blachowicz, editors of the Tools for Teaching Literacy series. Furthermore, we are grateful to those who lent their time and expertise to the task of reviewing drafts of our manuscript. Their feedback provided support and direction, both invaluable contributions to our work. In addition, we thank those who generously granted us permission to reproduce or adapt their materials for this text. As we have talked about this work with our colleagues in the field, all of whom have inspired and informed us, we have appreciated their thoughtful feedback on our ideas as well as their support. As always, we learn more than words can say when we share in community with colleagues. This book got its start when Chris Jennison saw its potential in an article we published in *The Reading Teacher.* We are deeply indebted to him for his vision and encouragement.

Finally, we thank our families, who have provided the most tangible and long-lasting support of all.

CONTENTS

CHAPTER 1. Introduction   1

CHAPTER 2. The Learning Environment for Effective   11
            Literacy–Technology Integration

CHAPTER 3. Learning about Effective Technology Integration: 29
            A Guide for Teachers

CHAPTER 4. Planning for Literacy–Technology Integration   43

CHAPTER 5. Teaching Effectively with Technology   58

CHAPTER 6. Using Assessment to Inform Decision Making   76
            in the Technology-Enriched Learning Environment

CHAPTER 7. The Teacher as Change Agent in the Literacy–Technology   91
            Learning Environment

CHAPTER 8. The Impact of Technology on Our Journey as Teachers: 105
            Looking Back, Looking Forward

            A Glossary of Terms: New Words Associated   117
            with New Technologies

            Appendices: Tools for Thinking about Technology Integration   119

            References   135

            Index   143

CHAPTER 1

INTRODUCTION

HOW THE IDEA FOR THIS BOOK WAS BORN

In the fall of 2000, we embarked on a journey to better prepare our preservice teachers to integrate technology effectively into their work with children. At a time when most university budgets were shrinking, funds *were* available to purchase computer hardware and software, and the calls for faculty to integrate technology into their instruction were sounding louder and more frequently than ever. There was a feeling campuswide at the University of Minnesota that the student body needed preparation for an increasingly technological world and that the faculty needed to respond rapidly.

The context in which we found ourselves was not unlike that faced by many teachers today. National surveys, as well as our work with practicing teachers, reveal that many feel pressed by the expectation to integrate technology into their instruction and to meet the International Society for Technology in Education (ISTE) National Educational Technology Standards for Students (NETS•S) (International Society for Technology in Education, 2000–2005). Back in 2000, we often felt that the pressure to integrate technology left the questions of *how* and *why* unaddressed.

Throughout our journey, critical questions surfaced: What *is* purpose-driven, effective literacy–technology integration? What does it look like? Sound like? How do we most effectively integrate technology into the literacy curriculum at the elementary and preservice teacher education levels? How can we effectively meet the needs of *all* learners with the integration of technology? In what ways can reflective practice and ongoing assessment specific to technology integration inform instruction? How can we foster communication and collaboration among teachers at all levels?

1

The content of this book draws heavily on our teaching and research over the past several years. We have explicitly studied our own efforts and those of our preservice teachers, several of whom we have followed into their student-teaching experiences and first years of teaching.

In this book, we share journeys of teaching in the digital age—our journey of designing, implementing, and assessing instruction for preservice and inservice teachers and the journeys of the teachers with whom we have worked as they have done the same for their students. Throughout our journey, we have striven to:

> ➤ Provide quality literacy–technology integration experiences for our students.

> ➤ Support our colleagues in their efforts to provide quality literacy–technology integration experiences for their students.

> ➤ Continually increase our understanding of effective literacy–technology integration through our work.

At this point, we turn our attention to a central question: What *is* literacy–technology integration? In other words, how might we conceptualize the role of technology within current understandings of literacy and literacy instruction?

THE NATURE OF LITERACY–TECHNOLOGY INTEGRATION

Before entering the digital age, the technologies of movable type and the printing press had probably had the most profound impact on literacy worldwide. Today, information and communication technologies (ICTs) such as word processors, e-mail, CD-ROMs, digital video, and the Internet have resulted in another profound change in the way in which we learn, work, and play (Leu, 2000). Adults in the workplace are now expected to be facile with these new technologies as they access, interpret, compare and contrast, synthesize, and communicate ideas electronically. In almost all U.S. colleges and universities and in many high schools, it is now commonplace for teachers to expect an assignment to be word-processed, perhaps even submitted electronically rather than on paper; many assignments require the use of digital resources and modes of presentation. If you own a computer, it is likely that you do not consider it an advantage so much as a part of life. If you do not own one, it is likely that you often feel disadvantaged as you coordinate your schedule with that of the nearest library or lab, pay a fee for printing, and so on.

There are numerous ways in which our lives have changed and continue to do so as we integrate this convenience and its challenges into the fabric of our daily lives. Think for a moment about the last time you used your computer, if you have one. Was it during the last 24 hours? The last 12 hours? Or even the last few hours? How did you use your computer? Did you send an e-mail message to a friend or check to see whether you had received any messages? Did you check the location of a new place you wanted to visit? Did you then type the address into MapQuest in order to obtain driving directions? Did you search for a recipe you once owned but can no longer find? Did you check the collections at your local library to see whether a book you'd like to borrow has been returned? Did you insert a CD of family photos or music? Did you download clip art to use for a project? Perhaps you read the morning paper online or checked the weather forecast for your area. The possibilities are endless.

Although workplace literacy has been more quickly affected by ICTs than has classroom literacy, Leu (2000) suggests that literacy, technology, and literacy instruction are quickly converging. Today, teachers are challenged not only to integrate technology into traditional aspects of literacy instruction (i.e., book reading and paper-and-pencil writing), but also to engage students in emerging technological literacies (e.g., online reading and writing) (Leu, Mallette, Karchmer, & Kara-Soteriou, 2005). There are at least two important aspects of literacy–technology integration: (1) using technology to teach more effectively and enhance the learning of skills and strategies that *currently* make up a strong reading/language arts curriculum, and (2) effectively teaching and enhancing the learning of skills and strategies that make up the strong reading/language arts curriculum of the *future*.

Clearly, the impact of technology has numerous implications for literacy teaching and learning. Leu, Kinzer, Coiro, and Cammack (2004) highlight the central principles of the literacies emerging from the Internet and other ICTs, almost all of which require new teacher understandings and practical competencies. Three of these principles serve as a foundation for this book:

> ➢ New technologies are constantly changing.

> ➢ New technologies change the very nature of what it means to be literate.

> ➢ New technologies demand a new and more important role for teachers.

Characteristics of the New Technologies

The ways in which technology affects literacy teaching and learning are literally changing in classrooms across the United States *as you read this book*. This unprecedented rate of change, which will grow increasingly more rapid, points to new directions in teaching and calls for new conceptions of teacher education and continuing professional development. Citing Senge (1990), Fawcett and Snyder (1998) suggest that professional development related to technology integration must focus on "capacity building, where capacity is defined as the ability to continuously learn" (p. 122). In other words, preservice teacher preparation and inservice teacher professional development in the area of literacy–technology integration requires more than a focus on the information and communication technologies themselves. Just as important is a focus on strategies for learning about new technologies as they become available and strategies for making decisions about whether and how these technologies might enhance literacy learning for students.

Characteristics of the New Literacies

Consider the fact that learning about a new topic, perhaps in preparation to write a report, is no longer confined to gathering a collection of books and photocopied journal articles. Today's research requires the additional competencies of using search engines appropriately, reading web pages, making decisions about which links to follow, and comprehending and integrating information presented in a wider variety of formats than ever and in rapid succession or even simultaneously (e.g., onscreen text, graphics, streaming video and audio clips).

Initially, many believed that new technologies would simply require the transfer of traditional paper-and-pencil and book-based literacy skills and strategies to the computer keyboard and screen; however, research indicates that the new technologies require new literacy competencies. Just as *traditional literacy* can be broadly defined (to include reading, writing, listening, speaking, and critical thinking, for example), the new literacies emerging from new technologies are also expansive. Furthermore, the fact that these literacies are not yet completely known but emerging along with technological advances makes defining them a difficult proposition. The following definition, put forth by Leu, Kinzer, Coiro, and Cammack (2004), serves as a useful guide:

> The new literacies of the Internet and other ICTs include the skills, strategies, and dispositions necessary to successfully use and adapt to the rapidly changing information and communication technologies and contexts that continuously emerge in our world and influence all areas of our personal and professional lives. These new literacies allow us to use the Internet and other ICTs to identify important questions, locate information, critically evaluate the usefulness of that information, synthesize information to answer those questions, and then communicate the answers to others. (p. 1572)

As technology increasingly becomes an integral part of what we understand to be literacy, achieving literacy (i.e., becoming literate) will require a wider range of skills, greater skill sophistication, and the ability to apply these skills more quickly than ever (Leu, Kinzer, Coiro, & Cammack, 2004).

Characteristics of Teaching within the Context of Literacy–Technology Integration

One of the purposes of any type of technology is to alter the ways in which people function. In the classroom, the role of the teacher is more important, not less, as new technologies become more central to everyday literacy instruction (Leu,

Kinzer, Coiro, & Cammack, 2004), but the question of precisely *how* the role of the teacher becomes more important is a relatively new frontier. There is much to learn for teachers, teacher educators, and staff development professionals alike. As literacy teacher educators, we find ourselves deeply interested in promoting more dialogue among those responsible for preservice and inservice teacher education. It is in this vein of dialogue, community, and capacity building that we wrote this book.

TEACHER DEVELOPMENT FOR LITERACY–TECHNOLOGY INTEGRATION: A NEW PERSPECTIVE

According to the National Center for Education Statistics (2000), teacher preparation for technology integration is minimal; in 1999, most teachers reported feeling less than well prepared to use computers and the Internet for instruction. Two large studies revealed that even in "technology-rich" schools, many teachers have not yet begun to integrate technology into their teaching (Becker, Ravitz, & Wong, 1999; Cuban, 2001). Thus, calls for increased attention to this topic in teacher education programs have been issued by numerous organizations, including the U.S. Department of Education (Culp, Honey, & Mandinach, 2003), the International Reading Association (2002), and the National Council for the Accreditation of Teacher Education (NCATE; 1997). Of those responding to a national survey on technology practice and policy, 87% cited professional development as one of their highest priorities for the immediate future (Swanson, 2006).

Given the constantly evolving nature of technology, interactive communication among preservice and inservice teachers, professional development facilitators, and teacher educators is critical to providing meaningful technology-related experiences for all children. Traditionally, these communities have worked in isolation, like individuals on independent paths. As we move into the digital age, there is a compelling need for these communities to come together and create shared responsibility for and ownership of literacy instruction.

Teachers of teachers reside in many places. They are in the district office and in schools, coordinating and implementing professional development experiences; they are K–6 colleagues teaching across the hall, down the block, or in another state who correspond with you by e-mail; they are in universities and colleges across the country, teaching preservice teachers in literacy methods courses; they are cooperating teachers in field placements. We believe communication and collaboration among teachers in all of these settings will have a profound impact on student learning in the age of new literacies.

Based on the assumption that inservice teachers, preservice teachers, and teacher educators can learn from and teach one another, we use teacher stories in the form of description and reflection as a way of inviting you into an examination of your own unfolding story and ongoing professional development. In the following chapters, you will meet teachers we have learned from over the past several years. Six teachers with whom we have worked closely throughout our literacy–technology integration journey are Jon David, Laura, Darin, Leia, Jinna, and Gail.

Jon David

Jon David is in his fifth year as a second-grade teacher. The students in his suburban classroom actively engage in technology embedded within the curriculum. Jon David's efforts have been supported by building- and district-level support staff. He has also had access to a variety of hardware capabilities and useful software both in his classroom and in the building's computer lab. What is perhaps most striking about Jon David is his initiative in bringing technology into his teaching in meaningful ways. With regard to literacy–technology integration, Jon David describes himself as an advocate; he is viewed by his colleagues as a leader.

Laura

Laura is in her third year of teaching. She has taught in third grade and kindergarten in a suburban school with a technology-rich environment. Laura exhibits an awareness of the role of technology in differentiating instruction for all students. She demonstrates an "I can do it" attitude related to literacy–technology integration and effectively verbalizes her commitment to integrating technology for meaningful purposes, rather than just for the sake of doing so. In part, Laura credits her effective literacy–technology efforts to her collaboration with colleagues.

Darin

Over the course of 5 years, Darin has taught in three different settings. He began his career as a teacher in a third- through fifth-grade multiage classroom situated in a suburban school district with multiple resources for technology integration, then assumed the role of a sixth- through eighth-grade math and technology teacher at an urban alternative school with more limited resources. Currently, Darin is teaching sixth grade in an urban school located in another part of the country. Despite the changes in his teaching positions, Darin has remained committed to providing real-life learning experiences where technology is seamlessly embedded within and across content areas. He views himself as a leader in this area and has consistently demonstrated qualities that support this perspective.

Leia

In her third year of teaching, Leia initially taught a fifth-/sixth-grade multiage class and then moved to fifth grade. In her tenure as a teacher, she has expressed her appreciation for multiple resources. Leia's commitment to thoughtfully organizing and orchestrating meaningful technology-related learning opportunities for her students is admirable. It goes without saying that she takes her role as a facilitator of learning seriously in all areas, including literacy and technology.

Jinna

Jinna is in her third year of teaching. Each year, she has experienced a new grade level, from first through fifth grade. She has also experienced a variety of settings, including an inner-city school with limited technology resources and a suburban school with greater resources. Jinna can best be described as determined. When resources have been limited, she has sought ways to use technology to inform her instruction. She is to be applauded for her commitment to stay the course despite the obstacles she has encountered.

Gail

Gail has taught sixth grade for the past 3 years. Her school is equipped with resources to support her literacy–technology integration. Gail is enthusiastic about the potential of technology to affect student learning, and she is interested in providing learning opportunities that engage her learners. Gail has been described by a colleague as "the model of a supportive technology teacher and mentor."

These teachers and their classrooms represent a range of contextual features that affect decision making related to literacy–technology integration. For example, their class sizes vary, as does the percentage of their students who struggle with reading and writing and are learning English as a second language. They also differ in years of teaching experience as well as the quantity and quality of resources available to support their technology integration efforts. What these teachers have in common are classroom environments and instructional settings that reflect recent research on the effective teaching of reading and writing (Allington & Johnston, 2002; Gambrell, Morrow, Neuman, & Pressley, 1999; Pressley, Allington, Wharton-McDonald, Block, & Morrow, 2001). You will find that such best practices are an integral part of the examination of literacy–technology integration found in this book.

In the following chapters, we make reference to our journey in literacy–technology integration, a journey that continues. Furthermore, we address prominent themes that have emerged for us and for the teachers we've worked with over the last several years.

GUIDE TO UPCOMING CHAPTERS

Here is a brief look at the contents of the remaining chapters of this book. For each, we list some of the major questions that frame the chapter.

➤ *Chapter 2: The Learning Environment for Effective Literacy–Technology Integration.* What are the common characteristics of learning environments that support effective literacy–technology integration? Which teaching methods work best in technology-rich classrooms? In this chapter, we explore answers to these questions and others related to the general learning environment.

➤ *Chapter 3: Learning about Effective Technology Integration: A Guide for Teachers.* What are some effective literacy–technology integration learning opportunities for teachers? In this chapter, we present learning opportunities that teachers have found powerful in their professional development related to literacy–technology integration.

➤ *Chapter 4: Planning for Literacy–Technology Integration.* How have new technologies and associated new literacies changed the face of instructional planning? In this chapter, we examine the multiple aspects of planning, including the determination of what to teach and the utilization of resources.

➤ *Chapter 5: Teaching Effectively with Technology.* What competencies are associated with reading and communicating through the Internet and other ICTs? Our investigation of this question includes a look at comprehension strategy instruction and the writing process in the age of digital literacy.

➤ *Chapter 6: Using Assessment to Inform Decision Making in the Technology-Enriched Learning Environment.* How can you design assessments to provide information useful for your instruction? We discuss ways to effectively examine student work and the role of assessment in the ongoing cycle of instruction.

➤ *Chapter 7: The Teacher as Change Agent in the Literacy–Technology Learning Environment.* What does it mean to be a change agent, and why is this important in literacy–technology integrated classrooms? In this chapter, we describe the attributes, attitudes, and actions associated with teachers who act as change agents in literacy–technology integrated classrooms.

➤ *Chapter 8: The Impact of Technology on Our Journey as Teachers: Looking Back, Looking Forward.* What have we learned from working with teachers on literacy–technology integration efforts? Here, we reflect on our own experiences as well as those of our K–6 teacher colleagues and consider directions for the future of children acquiring new literacies.

SPECIAL FEATURES OF THIS BOOK

We would like to call attention to three features of this book designed to support your efforts in applying what you learn to your classroom instruction and ongoing professional development.

A Glossary of Terms: New Words Associated with New Technologies

You may recall a time when menus and servers were found in restaurants, tools were kept in the shed, and engines were associated with cars, not searches! Indeed, the new technologies of the Internet and other ICTs have contributed to a whole new lexicon. Simple definitions of key terms are found in the glossary at the end of this book.

Appendices: Tools for Thinking about Technology Integration

Also at the end of the book, you will find a collection of documents that can help guide learning for students and for teachers. Several of the forms described in this book can be found in this section.

Inquiry and Reflection: Turning What You Learn into Action

At the end of each chapter, you will find a section called Inquiry and Reflection. This section provides opportunities for you actively to use the ideas presented in the chapter in your journey of literacy–technology integration. Whether your journey began when you picked up this book or long ago, these experiences will help guide your exploration, goal setting, implementation, and reflection. Active participation in a study group is a meaningful way to enhance your instruction and engage in professional development; thus, we encourage you to form a study group that focuses on the contents of this book. We urge you and your colleagues to meet regularly, possibly at the close of each chapter, and to use your completed Inquiry and Reflection activities to stimulate discussion. If you form an online study group, we suggest weekly e-mail correspondence addressing these same issues.

A NOTE ABOUT OUR APPROACH

As you read this book, you will encounter recurring themes based on best practices for instructional planning, teaching, assessment, and reflection. Bear in mind that this book is about two related aspects of literacy education: literacy–technology integration and teacher professional development. Our purpose is to equip teachers, university instructors, and professional development facilitators with information and tools to support the continuing development of teachers as they prepare children for reading and writing in the 21st century.

In order to ensure that this information is useful within the context of rapidly changing technologies, we limit our references to software applications and websites that are current as of the writing of this book and are likely to maintain a high-quality existence for many years to come. Ultimately, this book is about teachers and how to fuel their ongoing professional growth in an age of extraordinary innovation.

INQUIRY AND REFLECTION

Begin the practice of keeping an *anecdotal log* to record your thoughts and ideas related to literacy–technology integration as they unfold and evolve. The log can take whatever form you like: a three-ring binder, a Word document, a file folder to keep loose pages. Decide on a physical format that will be convenient for jotting down ideas, and periodically review and reflect on your ideas. To establish the practice of keeping the log, set aside time during or after reading each chapter in this book to record information, ideas, and thoughts. Here are two prompts to get you started:

➤ Write down your hopes for literacy–technology integration in your classroom over the course of the next 3 months. Turn this list into one or more concrete goals.

➤ Write down your hopes for your personal professional development related to literacy–technology integration. Turn this list into one or more concrete goals.

CHAPTER 2

THE LEARNING ENVIRONMENT FOR EFFECTIVE LITERACY–TECHNOLOGY INTEGRATION

Educational technology needs to be understood not as an isolated event, but as a piece in the puzzle of how teachers teach and students learn.
—WENGLINSKI (2005)

It is 10:30 on a Monday morning and elementary school students all around the United States are engaged in literacy events. They are participating in sustained silent reading, engaging in literature-based discussions, and brainstorming ideas for the stories they will write. They are doing author studies, reviewing lists of spelling words, and constructing story maps based on recently read texts. They are practicing sight word reading, locating information in encyclopedias, and writing persuasive essays. They are reading big books, morning messages, and directions at the top of the page or the screen. They are writing with pencils, pens, and keyboards. They are illustrating with crayons and cursors. As the array of literacy tools has expanded, so has the landscape of ways in which conventional literacy activities come to life in the classroom.

In addition, there are the new Monday morning literacy events: working with the teacher to create a class webpage, working with a partner to create a PowerPoint presentation, reading a text that has been translated electronically into an English language learner's native language, talking with an adult mentor via e-mail, and posting responses to Mildred Taylor's *Roll of Thunder, Hear My Cry* (1976) to a discussion board that can be read and responded to by students across the country.

With so many possibilities, it is somewhat daunting to address the topic of creating a learning environment that supports effective literacy–technology integration, yet one of the most critical conversations we can have as a community of educators is that of *how to decide* among the vast array of possibilities. Toward that end, we begin this chapter by framing our perspective on meaningful, purpose-driven instruction, followed by a look at the National Educational Technology Standards for Students (NETS•S) put forth by the International Society for Technology in Education. We then describe 10 characteristics of learning environments that promote effective literacy–technology integration. Next, we investigate motivation, engagement, and learning in technology-rich classrooms and describe related instructional approaches. Last, but certainly not least, we address the role of the teacher in a learning environment that promotes literacy for the 21st century.

MEANINGFUL, PURPOSE-DRIVEN INSTRUCTION

Research shows wide variation in how teachers define and struggle to attain meaningful literacy–technology integration (Fisher, Lapp, & Flood, 2000; Karchmer, 2001; Richards, 2001). While the last 5 years have seen a marked increase in the number of classrooms that have regular access to computers and the Internet, a common question remains: What should teachers be doing with the technology? More specifically, how can we know when we are using technology in meaningful ways and toward suitable purposes? In order to answer these questions, we must first determine a set of classroom goals for effective literacy–technology integration.

In this regard, we focus on instruction that is meaningful and purpose-driven—driven by students' instructional needs and meaningful as in likely to address those instructional needs.

We believe the goals of technology integration in literacy should be aligned with the following sets of knowledge:

1. What we know about the development of skills and strategies related to paper-and-pencil literacy.

2. What you know about the specific needs of learners in a classroom, balanced with their specific strengths and current competencies.

3. What we are learning, both collectively as a field and individually in each of our classrooms, about the skills and strategies of new literacies.

> The NETS•S state that learning environments should prepare students to:
>
> - Communicate using a variety of media and formats.
> - Access and exchange information in a variety of ways.
> - Compile, organize, analyze, and synthesize information.
> - Draw conclusions and make generalizations based on information gathered.
> - Know content and be able to locate additional information as needed.
> - Become self-directed learners.
> - Collaborate and cooperate in team efforts.
> - Interact with others in ethical and appropriate ways.

FIGURE 2.1. The National Educational Technology Standards for Students (NETS•S). Reprinted with permission from the National Educational Technology Standards for Students: Connecting Curriculum and Technology, ©2000, ISTE® (International Society for Technology in Education), *iste@iste.org*, *www.iste.org*. All rights reserved.

The National Educational Technology Standards for Students

The standards for student learning set by the International Society for Technology in Education (*www.iste.org/standards*) provide a guide for meaningful instruction. These standards, listed in Figure 2.1, challenge teachers to take students beyond basic understanding to the levels of thought required to organize, evaluate, and communicate information. In addition, they focus on preparing students with the skills needed to direct their own learning and to work cooperatively as part of a team. Since a thorough comprehension of these standards is important to instructional planning, we address them in greater depth in Chapter 4. We present them here to serve as a foundation for developing the context within which instruction takes place—that is, the learning environment.

CHARACTERISTICS OF LEARNING ENVIRONMENTS THAT SUPPORT EFFECTIVE LITERACY–TECHNOLOGY INTEGRATION

Given the goals outlined above, we have found that effective literacy–technology integration often includes the following 10 characteristics:

> ➤ Integration of conventional and new literacies
> ➤ Critical thinking
> ➤ Promoting learning to learn
> ➤ Integration of literacy instruction with content-area instruction

> Attention to social interaction and collaboration

> Differentiation of instruction

> Equity of access to technology

> Emphasis on the classroom as a learning community

> Multifaceted preparation for instruction coupled with flexibility and responsiveness

> Preservation of fundamental features of exemplary print-based literacy instruction

We now turn to a more in-depth discussion of each of these characteristics.

Integration of Conventional and New Literacies

Perhaps what is most striking about technology when it is effectively integrated into the literacy curriculum is the degree to which it is *not* striking. In these classrooms, teachers move students cohesively between electronic and paper texts, having them read and write in a variety of genres in each medium. Technology is used for multiple purposes and to meet a wide range of student objectives, including those related to traditional or conventional literacy learning and those related to new literacies.

For example, after reading aloud *Cloudy with a Chance of Meatballs* (Barrett, 1978), Jon David informs students that they will be using ClarisWorks for Kids to create pictographs of breakfast precipitation. He then models this process for his students, using a think-aloud procedure. As he shows them how to make a capital letter on the keyboard, he says, "If the light is on, you'll have all capital letters. Why capitalize the *M* on Monday?" In this lesson, Jon David fosters understanding of the concept of capitalization along with the keyboarding mechanics of creating a capital letter, integrating conventional and new literacies.

As Leu and colleagues (2005) point out, instructional goals related to the new literacies build upon the instructional goals of traditional print-based literacies. A glimpse of the similarities and differences between the two sets of goals is found in the examples featured in Figure 2.2.

Critical Thinking

Some people refer to critical thinking applied to literacy as critical literacy, which is not only the ability to read and write, but also the ability to use reading and writing to think about, evaluate, and solve problems (Harris & Hodges, 1995). According to Gunning (2003), critical thinking includes questioning information, identifying multiple perspectives on a single idea or event, and understanding controversy. Proficient critical thinking is a key component of new literacies, due in part to the sheer volume of resources available online and the unrestricted nature of online

Conventional Literacy Goal	New Literacy Goal
Students will improve phonics skills.	Students will become familiar with finding the word reading software program on the server.
Students will do research and create a travel brochure for Antarctica after listening to *Mr. Popper's Penguins* (Atwater & Atwater, 1938) as a read-aloud.	Students will do online research and create a travel brochure for Antarctica using Microsoft Publisher after listening to *Mr. Popper's Penguins* as a read-aloud.
Students will build background knowledge prior to seeing a play about Amelia Earhart by using print sources to locate answers to intriguing questions about her.	Students will build background knowledge prior to seeing a play about Amelia Earhart by completing a website scavenger hunt on her.

FIGURE 2.2. Goals related to conventional literacy and new literacies.

publishing (Valmont, 2003). Critical thinking includes mindfulness that authors have histories and agendas that influence what they write, including the perspectives they bring and those that may be absent in their work.

Aspects of critical thinking relevant to new literacies include deciding which links to click on when reading a webpage, whether a webpage is providing the necessary information for a particular purpose, and whether the information presented is credible. With the relatively recent phenomenon of global communication and access to information written in other parts of the world afforded by new technologies, students must apply critical thinking skills as an integral part of literacy learning.

Promoting Learning to Learn

Related to critical thinking is the concept of learning to learn. The rapidly changing nature of technology requires learners to learn not only the information available at the present time, but also how to update their knowledge base continually. Indeed, the very literacy tools for acquiring and communicating information are rapidly changing. Thus, another dimension of learning to learn is being equipped and comfortable with the necessary skills for learning new formats for reading and writing.

Learning to learn is at the heart of the inquiry approach. *Inquiry* has been defined as the search for information or knowledge where the focus is on the path the learner takes to get to this understanding (Short et al., 1996). Inquiry is based on learner-generated questions that allow multiple learners to approach an area of study in unique, personally relevant ways. Furthermore, the inquiry process often involves sharing, collaborating, and reflecting with each other about the questions, problems, and solutions involved in inquiry.

Teachers foster a disposition toward inquiry when they model not only what they know, but also what they don't know, and when they think aloud or talk through their processes for learning. In a learning environment that embraces inquiry, teachers are companion inquirers who model the process for their students, including undertaking inquiries to answer questions for themselves. This is in keeping with Allington and Johnston's (2002) observation that exemplary teachers admit when their knowledge is limited and support inquiry and problem solving in their interactions with students. As students apply what they have learned to their own process of conceptualizing questions and exploring to find answers, they will engage in learning that is meaningful, purpose-driven, and marked by intrinsic motivation.

Integration of Literacy Instruction with Content-Area Instruction

Earlier, we noted that the effective infusion of technology is characterized by the integration of conventional and new literacies. Such learning environments are also characterized by curricular integration, specifically the integration of literacy instruction with content-area instruction.

For example, throughout the month of September and into the beginning of October, Jon David's students enjoy the company of quiet caterpillars resting in glass homes on a low shelf in the classroom. They also assume the role of scientists as they carefully record their observation of changes in the caterpillars over time. Once the caterpillars transform themselves into butterflies, each second grader has gathered many notes. In October, they combine their notes with the capabilities of presentation software to create a slideshow with text and graphics of the life cycle of the Monarch butterfly.

Allington and Johnston (2002) describe this type of curricular integration "across subjects, topics, and time" (p. 215) as fostering engagement and reducing curricular fragmentation. In Jon David's case, the connection between literacy and science contributes to his students' eagerness to learn and the academic outcome of that learning.

Attention to Social Interaction and Collaboration

Although it was predicted that computers in the classroom would stifle interpersonal and academic interaction, research indicates that the opposite is true. Both the amount and the complexity of interaction among students and between students and teachers can be enhanced when working with new technologies (Kamil, Intrator, & Kim, 2000). Although social interaction and collaboration are important elements of any classroom, they are central to the workings of an effective, technology-rich learning environment. From supporting their peers with technical difficulties to joining forces to develop a multimedia presentation, students are actively engaged in meaningful conversations within the context of literacy–technology integration.

We have observed that teachers who effectively integrate literacy and technology treat social interaction and grouping arrangements as an important part of the curriculum, not just a factor in classroom management. They use flexible grouping and cooperative learning to ensure that students learn how to rely on and support each other in their independent endeavors as well as how to work together toward a shared goal.

Differentiation of Instruction

Differentiated instruction is an approach intended to meet the individual needs of all learners as they engage in literacy-related learning experiences. Differentiated instruction means, among other things, "affirming that students have different learning needs, strengths, styles, interests, and preferences" (Heacox, 2002, p. 17) and has as its goal "to plan actively and consistently to help each learner move as far and as fast as possible along a learning continuum" (Tomlinson, 2003, p. 2). Broadly speaking, differentiated instruction includes attention to instructional methods and materials, practice opportunities, methods of assessment, topics used to address underlying content, pace of work, or any strategic combination of the above. By taking different routes for different children, the goal is to move all children to a place of meaningful, high-level learning.

Many teachers find technology helpful in reaching students who seem otherwise inaccessible. Furthermore, we have found that when students interact with new technologies, individual student strengths and weaknesses that have gone heretofore unnoticed may become apparent. Take Laura's description of a special education student in her classroom:

> "When this kid can do more of his word processing on the computer, he's going to soar, because he's got the ideas up here [tapping her temple], but physically can't write them on paper. He doesn't have the patience or the small-motor skills to do it, even in third grade."

Laura goes on to say:

> "Some kids will fly on the computer where they can't in the regular classroom."

Laura's comment reveals not only the effect technology can have on student learning, but also its potential impact on a teacher's ability to differentiate instruction.

Though differentiated instruction is often associated with struggling readers and writers, it is important to note that all students benefit from instruction that builds on their strengths and interests in order to maximize their learning. The Internet and other ICTs offer many supports to teachers and students, opening the door to learning opportunities specific to the needs and interests of individual students. An English language learner can access information about the solar system translated into her native Korean. A primary-grade student who is challenged by sight word recognition can practice with voice recognition software equipped with feedback features. An intermediate-grade student in search of more information on the experience of African Americans who were enslaved in the United States can access slave narratives online.

As a final word on differentiation, it is critical that teachers' expectations for academic performance remain high and that the type of instruction provided promotes a high level of academic performance (Taylor, Harris, Pearson, & Garcia, 1998). Too often, differentiation for students perceived as struggling or at risk consists of watered-down content presented at a slow pace. As a result, children who struggle with one or more aspects of reading and writing will continue to struggle and never catch up to their peers (Allington & Walmsley, 1995). One way to avoid this problem is to include all students, including struggling readers, English language learners, and those who speak nonstandard dialects of English, in the development of higher-order strategies for reading and communicating.

Another approach is to use assessment to identify specific areas of strength and weakness related to reading and writing, rather than assuming a student with difficulties struggles with all aspects of literacy. For example, a student who struggles with decoding may have a rich vocabulary to draw upon for comprehension. Finally, it is paramount that students receive equal access to technology, regardless of their current level of literacy achievement. Comprehension development and assessment are discussed in Chapters 5 and 6, respectively. The important issue of equalizing technology access is discussed in the next section.

Equity of Access to Technology

The term *digital divide* was coined to refer to the gap in access to computers existing between poor and affluent students and also between white students and students of color (Munroe, 2004). Fortunately, computer access is becoming much more equalized across socioeconomic and color lines (National Center for Education Statistics, 2000), but Labbo (2005) warns that the challenge now is to eliminate the divide that can exist in how technology is used in the classroom.

In some classrooms, access to the computer is reserved for those students who complete their paper-and-pencil assignments with time to spare. In others, use of the Internet for research or PowerPoint for report preparation is incorporated into projects considered appropriate only for the most competent readers and writers. In other settings, the Internet and computer software are available to all students but only as a choice, not a requirement, privileging those who come to school already interested in and likely somewhat competent with technology.

The International Reading Association (2000) lists "Equal access to technology" as one of the 10 rights of children to excellent reading instruction. In other words, meaningful technology integration involves all students, not just those who are interested in computers, come to school with a lot of computer experience, are gifted, or are struggling. Through careful instructional planning, teachers can provide *all* students with equal access to higher-level uses of technology in the classroom. For Darin, this has meant involving middle-grade students in an alternative school setting in an online stock market game, requiring the use of sophisticated economic and financial concepts, and watching them become one of the best teams in the game, as well as having elementary school students sign in each time they use the computer during free choice time so that he can monitor and equalize computer access.

Emphasis on the Classroom as a Learning Community

Much has been written about the importance of creating a sense of community in the classroom, especially with regard to the rich diversity in culture, language, and home life that children bring to school (Au, 2002). A strong learning community integrates important aspects of each community member's history, culture, language, and prior knowledge. These aspects come together when opportunities for social interaction, collaboration, and personal representation are a deliberate part of the instructional planning process—in other words, when teachers are not only interested in students' voices but deliberate in designing ways to express them safely and respectfully.

Research indicates that the environment for literacy learning is strengthened considerably when there is a solid partnership between home and school (Edwards, Pleasants, & Franklin, 1999; Shockley, Michalove, & Allen, 1995; Taylor & Pearson, 2002). As children see their experiences at home embedded within the school day, specifically relating to literacy and technology, they are more effectively able to make connections between these two communities. Likewise, when teachers have knowledge of students and their home activities, they are better equipped to make wise decisions about how to embed technology in the curriculum.

Teachers are using innovative approaches to build and strengthen home–school partnerships, including the development of class webpages with weekly or monthly updates on what children are learning at school and how parents can support their learning at home, e-mail for immediate and convenient communication between home and school, and the use of video clips in presentations to parents to provide a window into the school day. Techniques such as these should not replace personal phone calls, handwritten notes, and hard copies of information, as many families do not own computers and/or do not value the Internet as a way of communicating with schools. Teachers who effectively work with parents to bring school into the home and home into the school use a variety of techniques.

In addition to seeing their home communities reflected in their classroom communities, teachers and students in many classrooms are rethinking the way in which they define their learning community from a global perspective. The Internet affords teachers and children a multicultural worldview at their fingertips.

At any given moment, the door is open for reading about and seeing firsthand the realities of other cultures.

Multifaceted Preparation for Instruction Coupled with Flexibility and Responsiveness

One way in which technology affects teachers' lives is in the area of instructional preparation (Coiro, 2005a; Wepner & Tao, 2002). Prior to lesson delivery, teachers routinely spend time reviewing websites, collaborating with technology support personnel, planning for teaching both content and process related to new literacies, and creating materials such as learning guides to support students as they apply what they've learned. They then make careful observations during their instruction to determine whether and how they need to adjust their teaching. For example, Laura observed during a lesson that a student was unable to read the information before him on the computer screen. She helped him find another website, one with a lower readability level, that she had encountered during her preparation.

For Jon David, much of the work his students do in the fall with technology is designed to prepare them for what they will do in the spring. He uses his anecdotal log to sketch out a plan and develops specific lessons accordingly. He regularly consults online lesson plans and seeks out workshops as part of his preparation for instruction. Like Laura, he maintains flexibility when his plans are interrupted. On more than one occasion, system difficulties have resulted in slow Internet access for children in the computer lab, leading Jon David to abandon his preferred plan in favor of a backup. He is constantly doing a cost–benefit analysis as he makes decisions about the best use of his students' instructional time, sometimes determining in the moment that the time lost waiting for online connections isn't worth the potential learning that will occur.

Preservation of Fundamental Features of Exemplary Print-Based Literacy Instruction

As previously stated, the goals of literacy–technology integration should be aligned with what we know about the development of traditional literacy skills and strategies. At this point, we want to emphasize that the integration of technology into literacy instruction should contribute to and enhance, not replace or detract from, aspects of exemplary literacy learning environments as described in the research literature. While many of the characteristics of learning environments that support effective literacy–technology integration parallel what has been found in studies of effective print-based literacy instruction, it is important to note other dimensions of effective literacy instruction that have not yet been discussed. In Figure 2.3, we list certain aspects of evidence-based exemplary literacy instruction that should be an integral part of all classrooms.

1. High quantity of quality texts for children to read at both their independent and instructional levels (Gambrell & Mazzoni, 1999; Worthy & Roser, 2004).
2. Long periods of time spent by children reading independently (Anderson, 1996; Worthy, Broaddus, & Ivey, 2001).
3. Direct teacher instruction in decoding, vocabulary, and comprehension strategies along with scaffolding to promote independence (Beck, McKeown, & Kucan, 2002; National Reading Panel, 2000; Scott, 2004; Taylor & Pearson, 2002).
4. Variation in assessment techniques to inform instruction (Gambrell & Mazzoni, 1999).
5. Integration of skills instruction with more holistic reading and writing endeavors (Pressley et al., 2001).
6. Integration of reading and writing instruction (Pressley et al., 2001).
7. High expectations for all students (Allington & Johnston, 2002; Pressley et al., 2001).

FIGURE 2.3. Seven fundamental features of exemplary print-based literacy instruction.

MOTIVATION, ENGAGEMENT, AND LEARNING

It comes as no surprise that students learn more when they are actively engaged in the learning process rather than passive bystanders. Active engagement may involve physical movement and/or verbal interaction and always involves wheels turning in the brain—the student's cognitive processing of information that will become his or her own.

It is probably also not surprising that technology can have a positive impact on student motivation and factors related to motivation such as enjoyment of schoolwork, persistence, and time on task (Kamil et al., 2000). Several factors contribute to motivation in literacy learning, including self-efficacy, curiosity, perceived importance of reading, and, of course, enjoyment (Guthrie & Wigfield, 2000). In a thorough summary of research in the area of motivation, Pressley (1998) states that elements contributing to student interest in and motivation for literacy learning are access to interesting texts, integration of literacy instruction with content-area instruction, and freedom of choice. He further states that students in effective learning environments receive the following messages: "Trying hard fosters achievement and intelligence; failure is a natural part of learning; being best is not what school is about, getting better is" (p. 236).

Many students find computers enjoyable. The Internet and other ICTs can be very engaging, sometimes increasing student self-efficacy or belief in ability to read and write. While technology can be inherently motivating for students, we have found that teachers who effectively integrate literacy instruction with technology are able to distinguish among motivation, engagement, and learning, keeping their eyes trained on the ultimate goal of learning.

ENVISIONING NEW LEARNING ENVIRONMENTS

The NETS•S call for the incorporation of elements of new learning environments into the classroom. Located on the ISTE website is a table, reproduced in Figure 2.4, contrasting characteristics of traditional and new learning environments.

Characteristics of new learning environments reflect a constructivist approach to teaching and learning. Teachers actively engage students in their own learning by informing them of the purposes of their work, which are authentic and meaningful, and use modeling, explanation, and discussion to move students toward self-regulation of learning and independence (Vygotsky, 1978).

Recent studies of technology integration indicate that traditional approaches to teaching, in which the teacher is the single knower who dispenses knowledge to his or her students, must give way to an approach in which the knowledge children contribute to the learning process is not only valued, but also seen as critical to the learning that takes place in the classroom (Kist, 2005; Munroe, 2004; Wenglinsky, 2005). With this in mind, we now discuss specific instructional approaches that promote learning with technology.

Approaches to Instruction

Two related concepts provide an important foundation for our discussion of instructional approaches: *scaffolding* and *the gradual release of responsibility*.

Traditional learning environments	New learning environments
• Teacher-centered instruction	• Student-centered learning
• Single-sense stimulation	• Multisensory stimulation
• Single-path progression	• Multipath progression
• Single media	• Multimedia
• Isolated work	• Collaborative work
• Information delivery	• Information exchange
• Passive learning	• Active/exploratory/inquiry-based learning
• Factual, knowledge-based learning	• Critical thinking and informed decision making
• Reactive response	• Proactive/planned action
• Isolated, artificial context	• Authentic, real-world context

FIGURE 2.4. A comparison of traditional learning environments with new learning environments. Reprinted with permission from the National Educational Technology Standards for Students: Connecting Curriculum and Technology, copyright ©2000, ISTE® (International Society for Technology in Education), *iste@iste.org, www.iste.org*. All rights reserved.

Scaffolding means providing the right kind of support at the right time and meeting students in their zones of proximal development. Vygotsky's (1978) concept of the zone of proximal development is well described by Graves, Juel, and Graves (2004):

> According to Vygotsky, at any particular point in time, children have a circumscribed zone of development, a range within which they can learn. At one end of this range are learning tasks that they can complete independently; at the other end are learning tasks that they cannot complete, even with assistance. In between these two extremes is the zone most productive for learning, the range of tasks in which children can achieve *if* they are assisted by a more knowledgeable or more competent other. (p. 60)

Pearson and Gallagher's (1983) gradual release of responsibility model provides a useful way to think about teaching as an act of moving students toward independence. The model represents movement through three phases along a continuum: all teacher responsibility, shared responsibility between the teacher and the student, and, finally, all student responsibility. In this model, teacher instruction and modeling, for which the teacher holds primary responsibility, gradually gives way to student practice and application, for which the student assumes primary responsibility (Au & Raphael, 1998). Scaffolding, or support that fades over time, is the critical bridge between student dependence and student independence. Furthermore, since students often scaffold one another's learning, a context of social interaction is key.

We now take a closer look at four specific ways (teacher explicit instruction, teacher modeling, think-aloud, and interactive demonstration) to teach within the context of providing instructional scaffolds and gradually releasing responsibility; you will see how these techniques can be used in various combinations based on the particular lesson and students' prior experience with the concepts being taught.

Imagine a multilevel second-/third-grade classroom in which students are working in small groups on author studies. In addition to searching for a breadth of information on each author, each group has come up with one specific question related to a unique aspect of the author's style. One group is studying Eric Carle and has chosen as its focus question "How does Eric Carle learn the things about nature that he writes about and illustrates?" The teacher, Maria, uses this question to teach a lesson on one aspect of searching the Internet—making predictions about which website is likely to provide the best answer to your question. She will begin teaching this strategy with Yahooligans, a search engine designed for kids. Her students are familiar with Yahooligans, having browsed the home page in pairs and reported back to the class on something interesting that they found, but they have never conducted a search. Maria has a set of laptops and a wireless system to allow for online access. Her laptop is connected to a projection system with a large screen. As you will notice, different approaches to instruction involve the technology in different ways.

Teacher Explicit Instruction

As its name implies, explicit instruction means *telling* students what you want them to know. Prior to teaching, Maria has had each group boot up its laptop, where the Yahooligans search engine has been bookmarked. After telling her students that it is time to listen, she explains:

> "When you sit down at the computer, you will see the familiar icon for the search engine. When you click it, the Yahooligans home page will come up on your screen. Since you are doing a search to find specific information, you will go directly to the Search box and type in the name of the author you're studying. Then you will click on the Search button. The next screen will show you a list of links. These links will take you to websites that may or may not have the answers you're looking for."
>
> [Maria pauses to take any questions that students have before proceeding.]
>
> "You could click every link on the list and then read through each website, but that would take a long time. A better strategy for finding the information you need is to read the name of each link as well as any other information about the link that appears on the screen. Think about what you've read and ask yourself, 'Does this link sound like it will have the information I need?' In other words, make a prediction, yes or no, about whether each link is useful for you to look at. Only click on the links that you predict will have the information you need. I will give you a guide called 'Predicting the Usefulness of Web Links' to help you with this activity. You will use it to direct your work."
>
> [Maria clicks on a direct copy of the guide that sits on her desktop and displays it on the large screen (see Figure 2.5). She uses her cursor to point to the left column, where she tells her students they will write down the names of the links. She then points to the boxes to the right of each line and explains that this is where students will put a check mark in the column for yes or no as they predict the usefulness of each link.]
>
> "When you are done, you will rate your predictions by answering these questions: Did we get a lot of information to answer our question? Did we get some information to answer our question? Did we get little or no information to answer our question? Write *a lot*, *some*, or *none* to describe how much information each link provided."

Teacher Modeling

Modeling refers to *showing* students what you want them to know and be able to do by doing it yourself. Here, Maria adds to her thorough explanation a model for

Name: _____ Date: _____

Search engine: _____ Topic: _____

Search question: _____

Name of Link	Prediction Question		Rate Your Predictions
	Do I think I will find the answer to my question if I click on this link?		Rate the usefulness of the websites you visited by filling in A LOT, SOME, or NONE. This link took me to a website where I found:
	YES	NO	A LOT of the information I needed. SOME of the information I needed. NONE of the information I needed.
1.			
2.			
3.			

FIGURE 2.5. Predicting usefulness of web links.

students to connect to the explanation. With the Yahooligans home page projected onto the large screen, she types "Eric Carle" into the Search box and clicks the Search button. When the links appear, she types their names into her electronic version of the guide. She proceeds to say:

> "Since I think the first two links will have the most information, I am going to check yes for those links and no for the third link."

She then clicks the first link and scrolls down the page. The children see her eyes scan from top to bottom.

> "Based on the headings I see, I think my prediction may be correct, but I will have to read in detail to be sure. That is what you will do in your groups. Are there any questions?"

Think-Aloud

In this approach, the teacher says what he or she is thinking as he or she engages in the task that is being taught. The think-aloud procedure takes modeling one step further, providing students with a window to what is going on in the teacher's head as he or she completes a task. Take Maria's direct explanation and modeling and add the following teacher talk when three links appear on the screen:

> "Well, the first link is called 'Eric Carle Author Study,' and it says, 'includes a list of his books and excerpts from an interview with the author' [http://search.yahooligans.yahoo.com/search/ligans?p=Eric+Carle]. The second link is called 'Eric Carle,' and it says, 'find answers to many of your questions for the author of *The Very Hungry Caterpillar* and many more books!' The third link is called 'Simon Says Kids,' and it says, 'this interactive site focuses on series like *Blue's Clues*, *Henry and Mudge*, and *Rugrats*, and new titles by authors like Phyllis Reynolds Naylor and illustrators like Eric Carle.' I think the first two links are the best ones because Eric Carle's name is the name of the website and the description is just about him. The third website seems to include a lot of authors, not just Eric Carle, so it may not have as much about him."

Interactive Demonstration

Labbo, Reinking, and McKenna (1999) suggest interactive demonstration as a robust teaching technique that includes explanation, modeling, and immediate student involvement. With this approach, students interact with new literacies concepts as they first learn about them. Maria can make her lesson interactive by including the group work within the fabric of the lesson itself, rather than saving the application until after the lesson. When the three links to information about Eric Carle appear, she can give her students 5 minutes to read the information in their small groups and discuss their thoughts about which links might be the best ones to visit. She can then ask them to share their thoughts and use their responses as a springboard for what she is teaching.

In highly interactive classrooms, student modeling often takes the place of teacher modeling, as knowledgeable students support their peers' learning. Similarly, student think-aloud can be an effective alternative to teacher think-aloud, as students are frequently intrigued by what their peers have to say. When students think aloud it can be beneficial to other students who hear the think-aloud and to the student thinking aloud, as he or she takes the time to verbalize the thought processes that are driving his or her reading strategies and understandings of text (Kucan & Beck, 1997). Furthermore, teachers can learn a lot about students' cognitive processing when students engage in think-alouds as they navigate and read online text (Kymes, 2005).

We want to discuss two aspects of Maria's instruction that can be used in conjunction with any or all of the techniques we've just discussed: *cooperative learning* and *learning guides*. Cooperative learning (Johnson, Johnson, & Holubec, 1991) involves having small groups of two to five students work together after receiving instruction from the teacher. In these groups, students work toward a shared goal, such as making predictions about websites, reading information found on those websites, and evaluating initial predictions. A critical feature of cooperative learning is that *all* group members work to ensure that *each* group member is progressing toward full understanding of the concept being taught. In other words, this is not a group in which one student does the work for everyone else or students individually do what each of them is already good at; rather, group roles are often assigned and rotated among group members. Johnson and Johnson (2004) assert that new technologies both support and are optimized by cooperative forms of learning.

We use the term *learning guide*, as exemplified in Figure 2.5, to refer to documents that support student learning. In Maria's lesson, students used a sheet called "Predicting the Usefulness of Web Links," which was designed specifically to assist students in learning about concepts related to navigating the Internet. Unlike handouts designed to assess mastery of concept knowledge, learning guides act as scaffolds for student learning by systematically engaging students in each step of a thought process.

The guide sheet that Maria used was in paper form so that her students could handwrite what they saw on the computer screen. For students who can easily handle multiple open documents, learning guides can be used electronically. Maria prepared her learning guide for use in a variety of lessons and with the intent of adding to its sophistication. Once students become adept at rating the usefulness of websites, for example, she will add her "Make a Plan" component, which will require them to determine a plan for continuing their research based on the degree to which their Internet search has been successful.

THE TEACHER AS CHANGE AGENT

By now, it is clear that the integration of technology into literacy instruction is not business as usual. Rather, it requires a change in the teacher's role in the classroom and in his or her approach to learning about and implementing innovation. In order to be a change agent in your classroom, you will first need to become a *changed* agent. In other words, you must be willing to explore teaching in ways that may be new and different and to learn as you go.

On this journey, your collaboration and communication with other teachers will be invaluable, whether they are colleagues in your district, classmates in a workshop or course, or teachers across the world who share with you access to the Internet and a passion for taking their students to new frontiers of learning. You will have the opportunity to use what you already know, not as a constraint to change but as the solid ground from which you imagine and explore, all the while having confidence in your thoughtful decision making.

Finally, this journey is a tremendous stride in your ongoing personal professional development—that is, learning that is in tune with your specific teaching strengths, teaching goals, and classroom realities. In the next chapter, we explore approaches to teacher development in the area of literacy–technology integration.

INQUIRY AND REFLECTION

In this chapter, we presented 10 characteristics of learning environments that support effective literacy–technology integration. Use the grid provided in Appendix A, Examining My Teaching Environment for Characteristics That Support Effective Literacy–Technology Integration, to describe the way(s) in which these characteristics are evident in your teaching setting; then set goals related to increasing the presence of these characteristics in your instructional environment. Develop a timeline for goal achievement in your anecdotal log.

CHAPTER 3

LEARNING ABOUT EFFECTIVE TECHNOLOGY INTEGRATION

A Guide for Teachers

As discussed in Chapter 1, the new information and communication technologies and the new literacies they require have implications for changing teaching practice. In this chapter, we address your personal professional development relative to literacy–technology integration. Recent research and theory on teacher professional development highlight as central teacher ownership and investment to the improvement of classroom practice (Ball & Cohen, 1999; Borko, Davinroy, Bliem, & Cumbo, 2000). No matter how important others may think a particular endeavor is relative to the improvement of teaching, what is paramount is that the teacher views this endeavor as important. Furthermore, it is now understood that teachers benefit from professional development time frames and structures that allow them to study, observe, apply, analyze, and reflect on instructional practice over time and in collaboration with colleagues (Commeyras & DeGroff, 1998; Lyons & Pinnell, 2001).

With respect to technology integration, new models of professional development are particularly important. Due to the ever-changing nature of technology, approaches to staff development focused on one person providing one way of teaching once and for all are becoming obsolete. We now recognize that capacity building is central to teacher education and professional development focused on literacy–technology integration. By *capacity building*, we mean "the ability to continuously learn" (Fawcett & Snyder, 1998, p. 122, citing Senge, 1990). Finally, it is likely that teachers' expertise and classroom resources vary more widely in the area of technology than in any other area of literacy instruction. Therefore, it is imperative that professional development efforts take into account teachers' multiple realities, rather than assuming one size fits all (Labbo & Reinking, 1999), and that teachers facilitate their own professional development.

In this chapter, we outline a range of concrete activities that you can select and tailor based on your level of experience with new technologies, your current instructional context, and your personal professional goals. In order to lay the foundation for these activities, we begin by discussing the impact of technology on the instructional cycle—that is, the phases of planning, teaching, assessment, and reflection. Whether you are reading this book alone or within a community, this chapter can serve as a guide to enhance the integration of technology into your classroom.

THE ROLE OF TECHNOLOGY IN THE INSTRUCTIONAL CYCLE

As you know, your work as a teacher is multifaceted. Although you devote most of the school day to interacting with students within the context of specific lessons, you spend countless hours on equally important aspects of teaching, including preparing for instruction and assessing its results. In fact, by using assessment to inform planning for instruction, you are able to link lessons, moving from short-term to long-term goals for student learning. You regularly engage in this cycle of instruction: planning for instruction, implementing instruction, assessing student learning to inform decision making, and engaging in reflection.

Research indicates that planning for instruction becomes more complex with the integration of technology (Karchmer, 2001; Watts Taffe & Gwinn, 2005). New technologies such as the Internet, interactive software, and interactive whiteboards can have a significant impact on instructional design, influencing the nature of your work during each phase of the instructional cycle. Our approach to literacy–technology integration is designed to support your integration of technology into each component of the instructional cycle. We propose the following phases for the instructional cycle in light of technology integration: planning for literacy–technology integration;

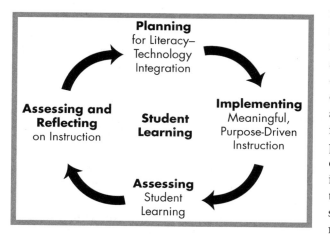

FIGURE 3.1. Phases of the instructional cycle.

implementing meaningful, purpose-driven instruction; assessing student learning; and assessing and reflecting on instruction. As illustrated in Figure 3.1, each phase of the instructional cycle revolves around student learning, which is at the heart of instructional design.

Technology affects the first phase of the instructional cycle—planning for literacy–technology integration—by increasing the number of options available in the design of lessons and units of study. In addition to your familiar resources for planning, you may now seek information and instructional ideas online or select software designed to enhance student understanding.

In the second phase—implementing meaningful, purpose-driven instruction—technology may be used to support teaching and learning directly. For example, students may use word processing or graphics software in the demonstration of reading comprehension, or they may explore various websites to collect information for a research report.

The purpose of the third phase—assessing student learning—is to inform decision making regarding future instructional plans and implementation. Here, you will determine to what degree your learning objectives were met and how you will provide further support to students who are still working toward understanding. At this point in the instructional cycle, technology may be the delivery tool for assessment (e.g., online testing) or one of the tools that students use to develop a final product to serve as evidence of learning. Preparing and delivering a PowerPoint presentation is one example of how technology is used to support the development of a final product.

The fourth phase of the instructional cycle—assessing and reflecting on instruction—focuses on self-assessment. As a responsive teacher, you engage in reflection throughout the instructional cycle, but it is often at the close of a lesson or unit that you are able to devote your full attention to assessing and reflecting on your instruction, then use this information to inform your planning for forthcoming instruction. Dialoguing with a colleague and writing in an anecdotal log are wonderful ways to make your self-assessment and reflection systematic. Talking with colleagues, both informally and during formal teacher study group sessions, greatly affects the depth of teacher reflection and allows for the exchange of a variety of perspectives and new ideas.

In the following section, we explore the impact of technology within each phase of the instructional cycle by looking at a specific unit of study designed for primary-grade students.

A Closer Look at the Instructional Cycle in Alicia's Second-Grade Classroom

Alicia is planning a unit of study designed to engage her second graders in reader response and align with her ongoing social studies unit The World and Me. Alicia begins her planning by determining her objectives:

> ➤ Students will recognize similarities and differences as they consider how children from various parts of the world engage in daily routines and make plans for their future.

> ➤ Students will recognize the characteristics of nonfiction evident in *Wake Up, World! A Day in the Life of Children Around the World* by Beatrice Hollyer (1999).

> ➤ Students will engage in and respond to *Wake Up, World! A Day in the Life of Children Around the World*. A particular emphasis will be placed on dreams for today and tomorrow.

> ➤ Students will increase their understanding of new technologies.

Now let's take a look at the phases of the instructional cycle relative to the instructional goals that focus on reader response and new technologies.

Planning for Literacy–Technology Integration

Alicia has selected *Wake Up, World! A Day in the Life of Children Around the World* because it builds on the background knowledge students are gaining during the unit The World and Me. Technology affects Alicia's planning as she engages in an online search for additional information about the featured countries in the book, including the United Kingdom, the United States of America, Brazil, Ghana, India, Russia, Vietnam, and Australia; she will share this information with students throughout the unit and during the remainder of the year. Alicia then schedules time to preview KidPix, a software program. Although Alicia has never used the software, she has heard from other teachers that it is kid-friendly and motivating to students. When she meets with the technology specialist to see firsthand the potential of KidPix, she learns that it may be used to present information using text, graphics, and voice in a slideshow format. Alicia is pleased to learn that her students are also able to add transitions between screens with sound effects and visuals. After she becomes familiar with the software, Alicia confirms its availability on multiple laptops. As she continues to become familiar with KidPix, she records information and ideas in her anecdotal log. Over the course of a few days, she begins to think more about her instructional objective related to new technologies, refining it. Her objective, "Students will increase their understanding of new technologies," becomes more specific: "Students will use KidPix, a presentation software that combines text, graphics, and voice, to develop a slide for inclusion in a class slideshow."

It is important to note that the process Alicia engages in is recursive in nature, especially related to the exploration of new technology. At the onset of the planning phase, Alicia has a general idea of her goals for students regarding technology integration—to heighten understanding of new technologies. When she discovers the capabilities of the software, her ideas expand to include student development of a class slideshow. Alicia is also aware of the need to monitor and adjust her instruction based on student learning; thus, she makes plans to follow achievement in an ongoing manner.

Implementing Meaningful, Purpose-Driven Instruction

Alicia introduces *Wake Up, World! A Day in the Life of Children Around the World* by identifying the author and describing the focus of the book: how eight children from eight countries experience life throughout a day. Alicia then turns to the world map at the beginning of the book and shows her students the featured children; she reads the meanings of the children's names and notes their homelands as identified in the text and linked to the map. Alicia tells the students that they will contribute to a similar world map, mounted in their classroom, by providing photographs of themselves to be linked to their homelands. Then Alicia begins to read aloud. When Alicia comes to the section "In My Dreams," she shares with her students each featured child's dream. Anusibuno from Ghana says:

> I dream of being a teacher when I grow up, or perhaps a photographer. I'd like to take pictures of ordinary people doing their everyday work and of children playing.

Cidinha, from Brazil, says:

> One day, I'd like to be a famous singer and dancer. For now, I wish I could have a doll. Sometimes I dream I'm sitting in the shade by a well and playing with a doll; sometimes I dream about the sea.

Alicia closes the first day of her unit by asking her students to think about their dreams. She poses a question designed to prompt reader response: What do you dream for today and for the future?

Over the course of the remaining days, Alicia and her students engage in meaningful learning opportunities that align with her objectives and meet the needs of each learner. They begin the second day of the unit by using paper and pencil to record their dreams. Alicia models the use of KidPix to create a concept map based on her dreams. A projection system displays her creation of bubbles as well as her demonstration of how to insert text into them. Her concept map, titled "Dreams," includes her name, Mrs. Johnson, in the center bubble, with the connecting bubbles including some of her dreams. After creating her concept map Alicia ranks her recorded dreams and selects one to feature in the slide she then creates to submit to the collaboratively developed class slideshow. After Alicia's demonstration, her students work in pairs assigned to a laptop to engage in the steps she modeled. First, students take their recorded dreams and develop a concept map using KidPix. Then they add text, rank their dreams, and decide on one to feature in the class slideshow. In the following days, students create slides of the dreams they chose. As a collaborative effort, students add transitions between slides and create a slideshow called "Our Dreams by Mrs. Johnson's Second Graders."

Assessing Student Learning

Alicia views assessment as an ongoing process across the unit of study. This process includes monitoring student engagement with the text, observing how and to what degree students recognize their commonalities with children from around the world, and examining student understanding of the characteristics of nonfiction evident in the selected book. One assessment focuses on each student's final KidPix slide as well as the process engaged in to create the slide. Alicia confers with students to learn how they determined the content of the text and how they created the supporting graphics for their slides. Each child collects all of his or her work related to the project in a folder, including initial thoughts and the concept map. These items spark additional questions that Alicia asks students as she confers with them. Students self-assess their individually developed slides for meaningful text, supporting graphics, and fluency of voice as they read their text. The complexity of the final product and the process by which it was completed is examined. Alicia uses a rubric that mirrors criteria presented on the student self-assessment to evaluate student performance. She allocates time for a class celebration of a job well done. As part of the celebration, students view the slideshow together. In the process, they consider similarities and differences between their responses and those of the featured children in *Wake Up, World! A Day in the Life of Children Around the World*. The following month, parents and other caregivers enjoy viewing the slideshow as well as the class world map while visiting the classroom for parent–teacher conferences.

Assessing and Reflecting on Instruction

Although the process of assessing and reflecting on instruction is ongoing, Alicia devotes additional time to this process at the close of the unit of study. She responds to a series of questions in her anecdotal log that she has begun to consistently ask herself. What went particularly well? Why? What will I do differently next time I implement a similar learning experience? Why? What was students' level of proficiency with the traditional literacy dimensions of the unit? With new literacies? What have I learned that will affect my design of future learning opportunities with embedded technology?

Alicia's thoughtful approach to each phase of the instructional cycle, a snapshot of which appears in Figure 3.2, is a significant part of her ongoing professional development.

In the next section, we share a wide range of learning opportunities designed to assist you as you plan for literacy–technology integration, implement meaning-

Planning for Literacy–Technology Integration	Implementing Meaningful, Purpose-Driven Instruction	Assessing Student Learning	Assessing and Reflecting on Instruction

• Select literature
• Locate additional information online to support book introduction
• Select software
• Practice using software to anticipate potential challenges
• Confirm availability of laptops and software
	• Introduce book and read aloud
	• Model the process of developing a slide
	  1. Record dreams
	  2. Develop concept map
	  3. Rank dreams
	  4. Create slide
		• Monitor student engagement
		• Observe levels of understanding
		• Engage students in self-assessment
			Critical questions to consider:
			• What went well?
			• Why?
			• What would I do differently next time?
			• Why?

FIGURE 3.2. A snapshot of the instructional cycle in Alicia's second-grade classroom.

ful, purpose-driven instruction, assess student learning, and assess and reflect on your teaching.

TEACHER LEARNING OPPORTUNITIES: GUIDING YOUR PROFESSIONAL DEVELOPMENT

The learning opportunities presented here were developed based on three principles. First and foremost, we are committed to focusing on *meaningful, purpose-driven literacy instruction*. For us, this means technology is thoughtfully embedded, rather than used for its own sake. Our second guiding principle, encouraging teachers to assume *a stance of critical thinking and reflection*, is especially important considering that with all instructional innovations, how they are used is key. Technology is rapidly changing, and staying abreast of it is a challenging task; thus, we emphasize the role of the teacher as an instructional decision maker. Third, *engagement in learning communities*, such as online book studies and conversations with colleagues, may enhance your effectiveness at the integration of technology into the curriculum. As this collaborative process unfolds, you and your colleagues will be challenged to consider new ways of conceptualizing the work you engage in.

In this section, we build upon our discussion of the role of technology in the instructional cycle as we describe hands-on, self-guided learning opportunities designed to fuel your personal professional development. We encourage you to engage in the opportunities that best meet your needs.

Planning for Literacy–Technology Integration

Website Review

You can visit literacy-related websites such as those of the International Reading Association (*www.reading.org*) and the National Council of Teachers of English (*www.ncte.org*) and examine the intent and credibility of other websites that might be useful in your teaching. As part of the review, you might consider the potential of each website to support planning and enhance your professional development. Many teachers find the website review chart in Appendix B helpful to their investigation. If you are working with a team of teachers, you can review websites together and post these reviews in a public place. A list of organizations that support student learning and teacher professional development, along with their website addresses, can be found in Appendix C.

Exploring WebQuests

One instructional resource available to you is the WebQuest. According to Leu, Leu, and Coiro (2004), teachers may use this model, developed by Bernie Dodge, to engage students in a meaningful learning opportunity via the Internet. A WebQuest opens with an introduction, which describes the purpose of the learning experience. Students are given steps for task completion, followed by a description of how each step is to be done. Next, students receive links to the required online information resources to complete the task. Students benefit from tips on how to organize the information they gather and engage in a closing activity designed to focus them on their learning. They may also be encouraged to expand their understanding of the initial area of study by examining connecting topics. As part of the closing activity, it is a good idea to provide students an opportunity to discuss with others, including their peers, what they have learned (Leu, Leu, & Coiro, 2004).

Although WebQuests can effectively embed technology in your curriculum, it is paramount that you critically examine them. Leu, Leu, and Coiro (2004) pose a series of questions to guide your WebQuest selection. We provide these questions in Appendix D. Be sure the WebQuest experience engages students in a learning opportunity that promotes the development of new literacies, rather than an activity that could be completed using paper and pencil. We encourage you to develop a WebQuest, either independently or collaboratively, that aligns with your curriculum. Submit your WebQuest for potential publication using the form found at *www.webquest.org*.

Learning about Internet Appropriate Use Policies

You can analyze district-adopted Internet appropriate use policies. If you are working with a team of teachers, discuss insights gained from a policy review. Consider how the policies support your efforts and those of your students and describe what the role of parents is in relationship to these policies.

Implementing Meaningful, Purpose-Driven Instruction

Engaging in Instructional Observations and Follow-Up Debriefing

We encourage you to invite an instructional coach, a colleague, and/or an administrator to facilitate lesson observation and debriefing with you. This learning experience provides you an opportunity to demonstrate your literacy–technology integration efforts during a lesson. You may choose to provide your observer with the lesson observation guide in Appendix E. Following the lesson, discuss with your observer the questions that appear in Figure 3.3. This conversation will provide you an opportunity to share your planning processes, instructional intentions, and reflections on the lesson. It goes without saying that this is a meaningful way for you to discuss your teaching and receive feedback in a situation free of high-stakes evaluation.

Assessing Student Learning

Examining Student Work

At the beginning of the school year, it is helpful to select two or three students representing a range of literacy achievement to follow closely. Throughout the year, you may collect copies of work representing these students' engagement in and learning from literacy–technology activities. As shown in Appendix F, each work sample is labeled with the student's name, the date, a brief lesson description, and teacher comments. Since our work with teachers involves their sharing across

---

1. What were your objectives? Do you feel as though you met them? Please explain.
2. What were the successes and challenges you encountered during the preparation, implementation, and/or evaluation of this lesson? (Encourage teacher to reflect on all three areas.)
3. What might you do differently if you were to implement this lesson again?
4. What influenced the lesson design, implementation, and/or evaluation?
5. How do you define meaningful technology integration?
6. Thinking about the lesson you just taught, how does it compare to your definition of meaningful technology integration?
7. Is there anything else you would like to share about this lesson?

FIGURE 3.3. Sample of questions to guide discussion after lesson observation.

school districts, we ask them to use pseudonyms when discussing students. We also provide them with a parental consent form for work sample collection. Student work samples help you consider the degree to which your instructional objectives have been met for these specific students and your related future instructional plans. We have found that they also help teachers articulate and better understand how their literacy–technology efforts are affecting student learning as they share in teacher focus group meetings. We recommend that you follow district policies when sharing student work with others.

When teachers spend the entire year following individual students who differ in early-year literacy achievement, they gain an understanding of students' multiple dimensions of learning and competency. Invariably, even first-year teachers see strengths in their lower-achieving students and sometimes previously unnoted weaknesses in their high-achieving students. This more nuanced way of seeing their students provides direction for teachers as they differentiate instruction so that *all* students can obtain the high-level literacy skills and strategies discussed in Chapter 2.

Assessing and Reflecting on Instruction

Writing Thoughts in an Anecdotal Log

Although you may record in a log your thoughts regarding the integration of technology into the curriculum throughout the instructional cycle, this activity is particularly important during the phase of assessing and reflecting on instruction. You may find this log most useful in the fall, when you are in the early stages of planning. The lack of structure invites you to use it as a drafting board, writing short notes to yourself, jotting down ideas, and even sketching pictures. Some of the ideas appearing in rough form in this log may make their way into the more structured instructional planning grid, to be presented shortly. In addition to providing a place for brainstorming, the log can be used to journal. Many teachers we work with find it useful to write about their teaching experiences, recording their recollections and reflections. If you are working with a team of teachers, thoughts recorded in the log could begin dialogue about ideas, teaching experiences, and reflections that stimulate thinking regarding new ways to integrate technology throughout the instructional cycle.

Connecting Phases of the Instructional Cycle

Using Instructional Planning Grids for Planning and Reflecting

One way for you to attend to technology integration is to use an instructional planning grid, provided in Appendix G. You can use this grid in two ways: (1) to stimulate and record technology integration plans for the upcoming month and (2) to record the technology integration efforts that have occurred in the preceding month. In this way, the grid can serve both prospective and retrospective functions.

Student Objectives: What is it that you want students to learn and be able to do as a result of the technology-related learning experience you plan and implement?

Preparation: What will you do in your role as teacher to gather knowledge about the technology-related learning opportunity you are designing?

Technology Applications: Software, websites, etc.

Evidence of Learning: Consider the performance of students based on student objectives as you ask, "To what degree have student objectives been met?"

Future Instructional Plans for Observed Students: Based on evidence of learning, what are your future instructional plans?

FIGURE 3.4. Definitions of instructional planning grid categories.

We designed the grid to align with what we know about effective instructional planning. Its five categories consist of student objectives, preparation, technology applications, evidence of learning, and future instructional plans. Each of these categories is defined in Figure 3.4.

Figure 3.5 shows an excerpt from third-grade teacher Laura's grid. We encourage you to update the grid in as much detail as you can at the start of each month of the school year. After the first month, reread what you wrote the month before and make changes to indicate what you have actually done.

If you are working with a team of teachers, introduce the instructional planning grid at a focus group meeting in the fall. At the beginning of each month, send an e-mail reminding teachers to type into the grid any plans they have for technology integration. It is beneficial to read updates as they come in and to print and save a copy of each update. If you have questions about something in a grid, we encourage you to request clarification from the teacher in a follow-up e-mail.

Building a Professional Development Community

In teacher focus group meetings, a powerful forum for dialogue, you can gather with colleagues to discuss challenges, rewards, questions, and other issues related to your technology integration. We have learned from teachers that these meetings serve as a catalyst for them to reflect on their experiences, both as they articulate them to others and as they consider what they hear others saying. Although the duration of meetings can vary, 60–90 minutes for a group of three to six teachers allows for substantive sharing while maintaining a well-paced conversation. It is a good idea to begin the school year by examining the technology environments in your classrooms and setting initial goals for technology integration. As the year progresses, you can move to examining student work in relation to instruction, refining goals, and reflecting on practice. We have found that careful consideration

Month	Student Objectives	Preparation	Technology Applications	Evidence of Learning: To what degree have objectives been met for observed students?	Future instructional plans for observed students
February	To find facts about wolves within their jigsaw category (e.g. habitat, food, types/species, communication, and families)	Researched the bookmarked sites about wolves and checked out others within the Ask Jeeves sites. Read nonfiction books in preparation and shared some with the students before using tech lab.	Internet Interactive games within the wolf sites	Each student was successful in finding at least three to eight facts within his or her category. The next day we got together in their category groups and decided on their top three facts to share with the rest of the class. Everyone participated and contributed to their groups as well as in the sharing. They all were very excited and interested in the topic. One student said she was done researching and with a little encouragement she continued and did find more information. Another student found his information and went on to help other students who were struggling with their category.	I feel that their use of research in the different housing of native people gave students the confidence to look for and search out the information they needed for this assignment. In the future I will need to make sure there are sites that will accommodate all levels of learners.

FIGURE 3.5. Excerpt from third-grade teacher Laura's instructional planning grid.

of student work in a community setting promotes learning about student progress and instruction.

Teacher meetings work best when one group member assumes the role of participant facilitator. In some cases, one person assumes this role for the length of the school year; in others, this role rotates among group members. The participant facilitator attends to three phases of the meeting process: preparation, facilitation, and reflection. Meeting preparation is focused on developing goals for the meeting and writing a meeting agenda. It can be useful to develop an activity for teachers to engage in, such as responding to a writing prompt, as a way of getting them ready for the meeting. Finally, it is important to think of questions that can be used to facilitate teacher discussion and shed light on what teachers are experiencing in their classrooms. A list of writing prompts that we've used to facilitate meetings across the school year appears in Figure 3.6.

Fall

1. What are your hopes for technology integration in the upcoming year?
2. How can you get started on reaching your goals?
3. What technology resources do you have available in the upcoming school year—hardware, software, Internet access, personnel?

Winter

The following questions refer to the students you are following as part of your participation in this project.

1. What did you learn about the progress of these specific students by reviewing their work?
2. What did you learn about your teaching from reviewing the work of these specific students?

Spring

1. In response to the question below, review your thoughts recorded in the fall regarding your hopes for technology integration. As you look back, how have your hopes evolved over the course of the year? What are your thoughts now?
2. At this point, what are your visions for the future?
3. What are some barriers you have faced as you have integrated technology into literacy instruction, and how have you overcome them?
4. Regarding the students you are following as part of this project, what did you learn about their progress by reviewing their work?
5. What did you learn about your teaching from reviewing the work of these specific students?

FIGURE 3.6. Writing prompts for teacher focus group meetings.

Meeting facilitation begins with sharing objectives and the agenda. If teachers have engaged in writing or another activity, such as collecting materials and student work related to technology integration experiences, the results can be used to launch teacher sharing. We have found that encouraging teachers to bring student work or instructional materials helps them tell their stories of using technology to support teaching and learning. We have also used our prepared questions to probe teachers' stories, keep discussion moving, and make sure that opportunities for teacher participation are equitable.

The final stage of the meeting process occurs after the meeting has come to a close. It is important to set aside post-meeting time to review your notes, think about what teachers said (and didn't say), and ponder how the group can best move forward. This reflection period is critical, as it allows time to interact with teachers' ideas, concerns, problems, questions, and triumphs. Using what's been learned from each meeting is a key component of planning for the next meeting.

The learning opportunities we've presented in this chapter are based on recent research on teacher professional development and studies of the improvement of teacher practice specific to literacy instruction (Ball & Cohen, 1999; Borko et al., 2000). They are designed to support you within the context of your classroom over the course of time and center on the questions and complexities you experience in your daily teaching life—those questions you identify as worthy of study. We hope you will find it possible to integrate these processes of individual inquiry and reflection with the processes of professional development for licensure maintenance that exist in your school district. In the forthcoming chapters, we take an in-depth look at the role of technology in planning (Chapter 4), instruction (Chapter 5), and assessment (Chapter 6).

INQUIRY AND REFLECTION

In this chapter, we presented hands-on, self-guided learning opportunities designed to fuel your personal professional development regarding literacy–technology integration. Select and tailor to your situation one of these learning opportunities that most effectively aligns with your level of experience with new technologies, your current instructional context, and your professional development goal(s). Throughout your engagement in this opportunity and upon its completion, record in your anecdotal log insights gained and how you plan to apply this learning to your teaching situation.

CHAPTER 4

PLANNING FOR LITERACY–TECHNOLOGY INTEGRATION

Traditional and New Literacies in Jon David's Second-Grade Classroom

In Chapter 1, you met second-grade teacher Jon David. Jon David has actively integrated technology into his instruction since his first year of teaching, and he highlights his animal reports project as one of the most meaningful literacy–technology experiences his students engage in. It is one of Jon David's favorite projects because it addresses several priority areas in his curriculum, including:

- ➤ Reading and writing expository/informational text
- ➤ Using the research process
- ➤ Note taking
- ➤ Working collaboratively
- ➤ Moving cohesively between paper and electronic texts
- ➤ Reading across websites
- ➤ Creating a multimedia report

The animal reports lesson progression involves a series of steps, as children use skills and strategies that characterize both traditional and new literacies. Working in teams of four or five, students research an animal of their choosing by consulting multiple sources of information. An important resource that all teams use is an encyclopedia on CD-ROM, which requires them to apply what they've learned about encyclopedia use, including the alphabetization of entries, as well as their knowledge of electronic reference materials. They search for information about the animal's physical characteristics, habitat, diet, life cycle, and other features they deem important. They then work together to create a report using word processing and graphics, with one team member taking primary responsibility for each component of the report. Children engage in this work for several weeks, during which time they navigate the digital encyclopedia and word processor with minimal assistance from Jon David and begin to learn the process of reading across websites.

A Look Behind the Scenes

It is clear that technology plays a vibrant role in Jon David's classroom without being its focus. The focus in Jon David's literacy curriculum is just that, the curriculum, with technology strategically integrated to support, enhance, and extend student learning. At the same time, one of the reasons these second graders create such high-quality animal reports is that technology integration begins early in the school year, which allows them to build on their acquisition of new literacies and the mechanics of using technology throughout the school year. This facilitates the gradual release of responsibility from Jon David to his students. Furthermore, technology is used for a variety of purposes, including those related to traditional literacy learning, new literacies, and content-area literacy. What has Jon David done to prepare for these effective integration efforts? How has he laid the groundwork for meaningful instruction and student success? How has he used technology to prepare for the integration of technology into his teaching?

While thoughtful and thorough preparation is the hallmark of all effective teachers, research indicates that it takes on new and multifaceted dimensions for those who successfully integrate technology into their instruction (Watts-Taffe & Gwinn, 2005; Wepner & Tao, 2002). In the past, observations of teacher practice focused on the instructional time spent with students. As we move forward, into the era of literacy–technology integration, it is equally important to focus on what teachers do both individually and in collaboration with others to *prepare* for this instructional time. In this chapter, we consider the dimensions of instructional planning that are most important for effective literacy–technology integration. These dimensions are aligned with the critical aspects of instructional planning and preparation identified by Danielson (1996), but we extend them to include the multiple facets of instructional preparation unique to the technology-rich classroom. Specifically, we address determining what to teach and optimizing available resources. Integrating assessment and reflection into the planning process will be discussed in Chapter 6.

WHAT DO I TEACH?

The first step in planning any lesson or series of lessons is determining your instructional objectives. As Durkin (2004, p. 21) wrote in one of the most popular reading methods textbooks ever published, the driving question is: "*Why* am I doing what I'm doing?" Jon David is exceptionally clear about his instructional objectives. He has devoted considerable time to learning and working with the reading and language arts standards upon which his Minnesota state grade-level objectives are based. Over time, Jon David is also developing a clear sense of the ways in which these literacy objectives dovetail with national technology objectives and how the two sets of objectives can build upon and reinforce one another. He also recognizes differences among students in their strengths and current limitations and uses this information to tailor his plans to individual needs. In this section, we discuss the role of standards and student characteristics in the determination of what to teach.

Becoming Familiar with Learning Standards

The age-old dilemma of determining what to teach has been addressed in part with the emergence of standards, or broad goals categorized by discipline, that describe what learners are expected to know and be able to do. Standards are designed to help teachers target their instruction and know what to look for in student learning. The No Child Left Behind (NCLB) Act of 2002 (Public Law 107-110), designed to close the achievement gap between the highest- and the lowest-performing students in the United States, establishes requirements for state standards in reading, mathematics, and science. In order to ensure that *all* students make adequate yearly progress toward achieving academic proficiency, NCLB also calls for regular assessments of student progress. Each of the major national professional organizations in literacy, mathematics, science, social studies, and technology has developed a set of standards that outline discipline-specific expectations for learning. Furthermore, the profiles for technology-literate students put forth by the International Society for Technology in Education (2000–2005) include performance indicators for technology-literate students at particular grade levels. These performance indicators for Grades K–2 and 3–5 are provided in Appendices H and I, respectively.

In 1996, the National Council of Teachers of English (NCTE) and the International Reading Association (IRA) collaborated to produce Standards for the English Language Arts (see Figure 4.1). These standards are designed to:

1. Students read a wide range of print and non-print texts to build an understanding of texts, of themselves, and of the cultures of the United States and the world; to acquire new information; to respond to the needs and demands of society and the workplace; and for personal fulfillment. Among these texts are fiction and nonfiction, classic and contemporary works.

2. Students read a wide range of literature from many periods in many genres to build an understanding of the many dimensions (e.g., philosophical, ethical, aesthetic) of human experience.

3. Students apply a wide range of strategies to comprehend, interpret, evaluate, and appreciate texts. They draw on their prior experience, their interactions with other readers and writers, their knowledge of word meaning and of other texts, their word identification strategies, and their understanding of textual features (e.g., sound–letter correspondence, sentence structure, context, graphics).

4. Students adjust their use of spoken, written, and visual language (e.g., conventions, style, vocabulary) to communicate effectively with a variety of audiences and for different purposes.

5. Students employ a wide range of strategies as they write and use different writing process elements appropriately to communicate with different audiences for a variety of purposes.

6. Students apply knowledge of language structure, language conventions (e.g., spelling and punctuation), media techniques, figurative language, and genre to create, critique, and discuss print and non-print texts.

7. Students conduct research on issues and interests by generating ideas and questions and by posing problems. They gather, evaluate, and synthesize data from a variety of sources (e.g., print and non-print texts, artifacts, people) to communicate their discoveries in ways that suit their purpose and audience.

8. Students use a variety of technology and information resources (e.g., libraries, databases, computer networks, video) to gather and synthesize information and to create and communicate knowledge.

9. Students develop an understanding of and respect for diversity in language use, patterns, and dialects across cultures, ethnic groups, geographic regions, and social roles.

10. Students whose first language is not English make use of their first language to develop competency in the English language arts and to develop understanding of content across the curriculum.

11. Students participate as knowledgeable, reflective, creative, and critical members of a variety of literacy communities.

12. Students use spoken, written, and visual language to accomplish their own purposes (e.g., for learning, enjoyment, persuasion, and the exchange of information).

FIGURE 4.1. The 12 Standards for the English Language Arts of the NCTE and the IRA. From National Council of Teachers of English and International Reading Association (1996). Copyright 1996 by the International Reading Association. Reprinted by permission.

> Bring to the forefront the literacy needs of today and of the future.

> Encourage consistency within and across schools at the district, state, and national levels.

> Articulate expectations for student learning shared by teachers around the United States.

Through Jon David's animal report project, children are working toward several of the NCTE/IRA goals. For example, Jon David's students seek and summarize information regarding the selected animals from both paper and electronic texts, as described in standard 8. The authors of the reports enhance their knowledge throughout the research process and share this knowledge with others through their word-processed reports.

Furthermore, the scope and depth of the animal report project addresses not only reading and writing standards, but also the national- and state-level Science Education Content Standards and several of the National Educational Technology Standards for Students, described in Chapter 2. Elements of the National Science Education Content Standards are addressed as Jon David's second graders develop an understanding of the characteristics, life cycles, and environments of the featured animals. With regard to technology standards, Jon David's students collect, organize, examine, and summarize information in a collaborative manner and share their multimedia reports with peers. As second graders, they are learning how the Internet and other information and communication technologies provide answers to their questions and the way in which to share these answers with others. The opportunity to explore new literacies will serve them well, especially considering the ever-changing nature of technology and its impact on literacy and content areas.

So you may ask, "How can I apply what I have learned from Jon David regarding planning for effective technology integration to my own teaching situation?" First, ask questions and seek information from district- and building-level staff regarding district technology integration goals. Second, learn about national and state standards. Your district-level colleagues, particularly curriculum specialists, may be helpful in your pursuit of this knowledge.

Using Teacher Knowledge of Students in Instructional Planning

Instructional planning reflects teacher knowledge of students and the ways in which they learn most effectively. Jon David considers students' cognitive, emotional, and social growth as he designs instruction. As in most classrooms, his students reflect a wide range of reading levels. Half of his students receive Title I reading instruction, and a few receive special education. In addition, some are learning English as a second language. As Jon David develops his instructional goals, he considers his students' responses to various instructional techniques. His goal is to meet students' needs and capitalize on their strengths.

As part of the instructional planning process, Jon David considers student interests and attitudes. In the fall, he gains information about his new students and their interests from the pages they submit for the class All About Me book. Using a computer, students create text and illustrations to describe important aspects of their lives such as their families and hobbies. As noted in the example in Figure 4.2, Michael identifies himself as a talented artist. Thus, opportunities to use software featuring drawing tools will most likely be motivating to him.

In addition to well-designed classroom-based activities, communicating with parents is an important part of gathering information about students, especially at the beginning of the year when initial planning is underway. Surveys such as the Family Survey of Children's Attitudes toward Reading, Writing, and Technology (see Appendix J) can be particularly useful. Using this survey, Jon David learned

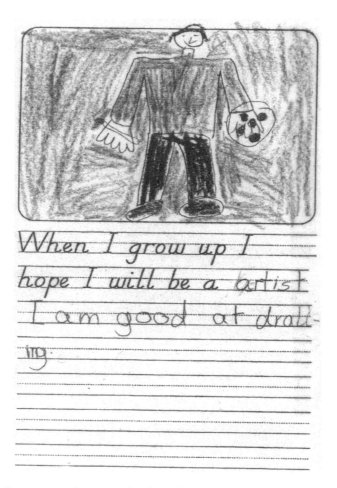

FIGURE 4.2. Excerpt from Michael's submission for the All About Me book.

that although Tiffany, a student receiving Title I support, was frustrated with reading and writing, she thoroughly enjoyed using the computer. This knowledge affirmed for Jon David his plan to incorporate the computer into Tiffany's reading and writing instruction. Since Jon David was interested in obtaining Tiffany's parents' perspectives at the end of the year, he asked Tiffany's mother to complete the survey a second time. She indicated that Tiffany's interest in reading and writing had increased and that she was now attempting to read independently at home and asking to be read to.

When determining what to teach, national goals, which are interpreted at state and district levels, must be coupled with knowledge of learners' needs. Once established, these instructional goals are most likely to be met when they are linked with the sufficient resources to carry them out.

WHAT ARE MY RESOURCES?

An important part of instructional planning is the identification and utilization of available resources. It is helpful to think of two types: teacher resources and student resources. Teacher resources are those people, materials, and sources of information that enable your instruction by helping you first to generate ideas and then to put those ideas into a coherent plan. Student resources are those people, materials, and sources of information that enable student learning within the context of specific lessons and longer units of study. In the following sections, we consider a variety of resources available to you and your students that can enhance learning and instruction in your classroom.

Teacher Resources

Getting to Know What's Available in Your Building and District

It may sound self-evident, but the first step on the path of effective literacy–technology integration is to learn exactly what resources your building and district have to support the integration of technology into your classroom. Perhaps you are in a building where new technologies are sprouting up all around you, individual classrooms are equipped with up-to-date hardware and high-speed Internet access, teachers "talk tech" in the lounge, and you feel at a loss to keep up with what others are doing. Or perhaps you are in a building with one computer in a corner of the library, a few pieces of software, and no one who can provide leadership in the best ways to make use of what is available. In either case, it is important to press forward in learning what is available. Most of the teachers we've worked with have used resources they never would have dreamed existed by simply asking what is available, how it works, and what it can be used for, then experimenting with it on their own.

It is also important to remember that human resources in the form of knowl-edgeable others—media specialists, computer lab teachers, classroom teacher col-leagues, and members of district technology committees—are just as important as the actual technology in helping you to learn how to make the most of technology in your classroom. Furthermore, you may find resources available through your district that are not available at the building level. Finally, knowing what isn't avail-able is just as important as knowing what is. Teachers who do not find the soft-ware, hardware, or Internet capabilities they need to optimize student learning often take leadership roles in helping buildings and districts acquire resources. It is a good idea to take time each fall to investigate what technology resources are available in the form of hardware, software, Internet access, and personnel.

Online Resources

Online resources are useful to all teachers, even those working with little or no computer access for their students. Jinna, a fifth-grade teacher in an alternative school, spent much of her first year of teaching waiting for her students to receive the promised computer and Internet access, but she began using the Internet to inform her instruction at the start of the year by finding information to assist her in getting literature circles up and running in her classroom and learning about local sites for potential field trips. As with all information on the Internet, it is important to remember that lesson plans, teaching ideas, and related materials may be posted by anyone, for any purpose. Not all of the teaching ideas posted online are grounded in research-based effective practice or national standards, and even high-quality ideas may not be well suited to your setting. Obviously, only you know your students, your resources, and your instructional goals, all of which will help you determine which ideas are worthy of pursuit.

Professional organizations tend to have up-to-date, trustworthy information. The IRA (*www.reading.org*) and the NCTE (*www.ncte.org*) provide a wealth of rich, high-quality resources, including lesson plans and student materials linked both to the IRA/NCTE standards and to specific literature or topics of study. You will also find links to peer-reviewed websites and listservs to continue your exploration. ReadWriteThink (*ReadWriteThink.org*), a collaborative effort of the IRA, the NCTE, and MarcoPolo, may be a particularly helpful resource as you seek to integrate the Internet meaningfully into your instruction. Biographies: Creating Timelines of a Life is an example of a lesson designed for intermediate-grade students that is available on this website (see Figure 4.3). This lesson leads students in the devel-opment of a timeline of a person of interest. In the process, students work collabor-atively to review various informational resources.

In addition to providing lesson ideas, the Internet can support dialogue among professionals. The RTEACHER listserv, for example, sponsored by the IRA, pro-vides a forum for K–12 educators to discuss issues related to literacy–technology integration.

FIGURE 4.3. ReadWriteThink website screenshot. This Biographies: Creating Timelines of a Life lesson plan provided by ReadWriteThink, a MarcoPolo website developed by the International Reading Association, the National Council of Teachers of English, and in partnership with the MCI Foundation. Copyright 2002–2006 by the National Council of Teachers of English and the International Reading Association. Reprinted by permission.

A list of professional organizations and agencies that will have links to the most up-to-date websites with valuable teaching ideas and professional development materials appears in Appendix C. In addition, many state departments of education have information specific to their standards on their websites to assist in your instruction and assessment.

Educational Software

Because software is routinely revised, updated, and replaced in concert with the expanding capabilities of hardware, an investigation of what you have at your disposal must include a critical review of its potential to enhance student learning in your classroom. Even within one aspect of literacy development, such as spelling, there are many types of software that vary in a number of dimensions. Wepner and Ray (2000) suggest several features of software design to consider when making decisions. We have listed these guidelines in the form of questions in Figure 4.4.

One piece of software Jon David used for the animal report project was the Golden Book Encyclopedia. In preparation for this unit, he spent time with the software to be sure that he could easily maneuver within it from place to place and to troubleshoot areas that might cause problems for his students. Wepner and Ray

---

- Are the activities and tasks within the program compelling enough to hold students' interest?
- Are the instructions clear, concise, and easy to follow without significant adult help?
- Are the graphics and sound of high quality, an integral part of the concepts and content taught, and appropriate for the age level intended?
- Does the content fit into or expand beyond expected student learning?
- Does the program stretch students' imagination and creativity beyond ordinary means?
- Does the program provide enough practice on important concepts, especially if a program that builds skills is needed?
- Does the program foster interaction and cooperative activities, especially if these are desired activities in the classroom?
- Is the text narrated so students can read the book or passage independently, and is the text highlighted as it is read so students can follow along?
- Does the program develop with students over the course of the year or accommodate differing ability or age levels?
- Are record-keeping or assessment features built into the program, especially if this is an important issue in providing accountability for technology use?
- Does the publisher provide a teacher's guide with lessons, ways to introduce the program to students, and supplementary materials to support implementation?
- Is there a printed copy of the book available for students to use independently?

FIGURE 4.4. Software design features to consider. From Wepner and Ray (2000). Copyright 2000 by the International Reading Association. Reprinted with permission of Shelly B. Wepner and the International Reading Association.

(2000) have several useful suggestions for preparing to use software with children, including the use of think-alouds during the lesson. Think-alouds can be used to show students how to use new software and where to seek help when they get stuck. It is also helpful to provide students with a poster featuring frequently asked questions about software and their answers, as well as time to process their experiences related to the use of the software during and after the lesson. Additional guidelines are captured by four of Wepner and Ray's (2000) key words—develop, identify, troubleshoot, and stretch—as outlined in Figure 4.5.

Jon David is a critical consumer who devotes a great deal of time to previewing and testing software and websites. During this process, he decides against as many as or more applications than he ultimately decides to use with his students. He then observes the ways in which his students interact with various technologies (e.g., storybook software, interactive whiteboards, websites), paying particular attention to whether they can use the technology easily, whether they are engaged by the technology, and whether and what they are learning. He also reflects on his experiences teaching with various technologies, ultimately deciding that the usefulness of some is outweighed by technical difficulties that cost valuable instructional time or lead to student frustration. Jon David has thrown away as many ideas for technology integration as he's held on to and works continually to refine those he keeps. While he is committed to effective, efficient technology use in his classroom, he doesn't let failure change his course if he believes that he can find the resources he needs to overcome obstacles.

Develop your own skills and confidence	• Read the manual, consult the teacher's guide, and check the publisher's website for answers to frequently asked questions and practical teaching ideas.
Identify unique features of software	• What can the software do that other instructional strategies cannot? • How can you capitalize on these features?
Troubleshoot potential problems	• What areas might cause difficulty for your students? • What questions will they have?
Stretch your imagination	• Think creatively and brainstorm ideas for unanticipated uses of the software. • Talk to other teachers. • Use your observations of students' interactions with the software to spark ideas.

FIGURE 4.5. Guidelines for preparing to use software with students. Adapted from Wepner and Ray (2000). Copyright 2000 by the International Reading Association. Adapted by permission.

Human Resources

Perhaps the most important resources you will find are people, some of whom will provide leadership and guidance based on their knowledge and experience with technology, some of whom will look to you for guidance and support, and most of whom will be similar to you in knowledge and experience and looking for a collegial community. The most obvious human resources are those who bring both teaching experience and knowledge of new technologies to professional roles in which they are charged specifically with providing assistance to teachers in technology integration efforts. Such resource personnel, who may be housed in your building or at the district level, can be very helpful.

In addition, fellow classroom teachers can provide ideas and be a source of communication and support relating to technology integration. Most teachers tell us that their colleagues, both locally and globally, are their most valued resources as they improve their practice in literacy–technology integration. As a seventh-/eighth-grade teacher who had very little technology available in his alternative school setting, Darin found that online colleagues teaching in similar settings were his best resources, helping him figure out ways to get more technology into his building as well as collaborating with him on lesson ideas.

Jon David has been fortunate to have a building technology specialist, with whom he collaborates on lesson ideas and who helps him with technical difficulties. Still, he has pursued additional guidance from the district technology specialist, attended workshops offered by the district, and regularly interfaced with the technology committee in his building, eventually becoming a member of this committee, when working on special projects such as creating a class website.

Student Resources

Now, let's consider resources that are available in the form of Internet access, personnel, and supporting materials for students.

Online Resources

Searching for information online is perhaps the most obvious new literacy we need to teach students. Jon David's students consulted online resources to complement the Golden Book Encyclopedia on CD-ROM because they learned that one source would not provide all of the information they needed. To add this component to the animal reports project, Jon David first needed to do a search of his own to identify possible websites for student use. As he searched, he kept the following criteria in mind:

> ➤ Is this website appropriate to the unit of study?
> ➤ Is this website appropriate to my students' reading levels?

> Is this website appropriate to my students' developmental levels?

> Is this website safe for children?

Yahooligans! (2002) encourages teachers to evaluate websites using criteria perhaps best described as the Four A's: Is the site Accessible? Accurate? Appropriate? Appealing? Accessibility focuses on availability of the site in its entirety, loading speed, and ease of navigation. Although the Internet is a meaningful source of information, it is important to recognize that anyone can create a webpage. Thus, it is critical to examine author credentials and the date on which information was posted, in conjunction with accuracy. Regarding appropriateness, it is important to consider the intended audience, language use, and topic specificity. Appeal focuses on the site's design and ease of use. A colorful, easy-to-follow site with well-placed graphics will most likely be motivating to students.

One of the most important aspects of critical literacy we can teach students in the age of the Internet is how to think about the information they read. It is vital that students learn to determine the likely credibility of the information posted on the Internet, especially as they enter the upper elementary and middle grades, when they are more likely to engage in independent searches in addition to visiting teacher-identified websites. In Jon David's project, second graders were learning how to find specific websites he had preselected, a skill laying the foundation for more sophisticated searching in later grades. Finally, almost all schools have Internet appropriate use policies in place so that teachers, students, and parents are aware of how students may and may not use the Internet in school. Such policies are designed to ensure the safety of children and to maintain the integrity of the school's academic program. It goes without saying that these policies must underlie all that you do with children and the Internet.

Human Resources

We cannot overstate that the most important resources for students as they navigate technology in the curriculum are their teachers. As you integrate technology into your instruction, students will look to you to learn both the mechanics of new technologies and the new literacies associated with them. Since it takes time to get a strong command of new technologies, it is very helpful to work with your building technology or media specialist when using new technology or when using familiar technology in a new way.

For example, one of the requirements of the animal reports project is to read and take notes on the information presented on a website, then to synthesize it with information found in a digital encyclopedia. Another requirement is to import a color photograph from a website to use as cover art for the report. Using illustrations to support text is a dimension of traditional literacy, but importing the graphic is a mechanical dimension of new literacies. Jon David is well equipped to teach his students how to take notes, synthesize across multiple texts, and create a written report. He feels less confident teaching his students how to import a graphic from an online source into their reports, so he seeks support from his building's technology specialist to provide this instruction for his students.

Jon David expects to take over this aspect of the project in the future; in the meantime, he supports himself with a scaffold, much the way we support students, and provides an enhanced learning opportunity for his students. This resource also frees up Jon David to spend most of his planning time on his areas of expertise: reading and writing instruction. Given how quickly technology changes, the best use of your time as a classroom teacher may not be in keeping up with mechanics, but in getting in the habit of collaboration with those who do have expertise in this area.

Students are also wonderful resources for each other in the exploration of technology, and this collaborative work is an essential component of the standards related to technology use. In Jon David's classroom, we see a commitment to fostering social interaction and establishing effective grouping patterns to facilitate learning. Methods of collaboration are often included in his student lesson objectives, establishing them as part of the curriculum. Over the years, through deliberate practice and observation, Jon David has become very skilled at establishing effective collaborative working arrangements for students as they interact with technology. Even when they are engaged in independent activities, his students routinely call upon one another for help. Just a brief visit to Jon David's classroom reveals that his students perceive themselves as part of a community. In Chapter 2, we discussed the importance of establishing a community in your classroom. Here we provide a specific idea for establishing an environment where children support and are supported by one another in their learning.

*Students as Procedural Coaches.*Even in the primary grades, children are old enough to teach their peers in more than a casual way. An approach used by many teachers is to spend time teaching a small group of children a routine, such as the mechanics of using new software, and then to have these students serve as team leaders or coaches for other children. When children have a question, they first consult their team leader, who coaches them through the process. Not only is this a good way to systematize working together, but it is also a meaningful way to build academic language skills in students as they teach their peers. By rotating leadership roles within the class, all students, regardless of their current achievement level in reading and writing, can experience the pride and increased learning that comes from teaching others.

Supporting Materials

An additional resource for students is material to guide or scaffold their use of technology. For example, Jon David created a note-taking sheet to guide students through the process of collecting information about their featured animals. Another such example is illustrated in Maria's author study featured in Chapter 2.

Such learning guides are useful for reading expository text in general but take on greater importance when reading expository text online. The creation of learning guides is an important dimension of the planning process. Teachers often find it most effective and efficient to create learning guides together, and some collaborate with the building technology specialist.

PUTTING IT ALL TOGETHER TO CREATE A PLAN FOR ACTION

An action plan provides a guide for teachers and includes instructional goals, based on standards and students, and the identification and use of resources (both teacher and student, online and human). It is apparent in Jon David's instructional planning that as the year progresses student tasks become increasingly difficult. For example, students' first exposure to technology was viewing a digital video created by Jon David introducing them to second grade; midway through the year, they are developing animal reports, which is a multilevel learning opportunity. This cohesive movement from the simple to the complex is facilitated by Jon David's systematic consideration of the various dimensions of planning that we have discussed in this chapter. Of course, to put it all together means weaving planning, instruction, and assessment. In Chapter 5, we address instruction.

INQUIRY AND REFLECTION

In this chapter, we discussed what to teach and the resources that support this instruction. Allocate time to identify online resources that can support you in your literacy–technology integration efforts. To guide you in your investigation, use the website review chart found in Appendix B. Record on the chart how the selected websites may support your planning for instruction, implementation of instruction, and personal professional development. Record in your anecdotal log what you have learned and how you will use this information in the near future.

CHAPTER 5

TEACHING EFFECTIVELY WITH TECHNOLOGY

Reading Electronic Text in First Grade

On a sunny April afternoon, Jonathan, a first grader, is reading an electronic text during free time. He has selected a story on CD-ROM. He carefully opens the CD case, removes the CD, and inserts the disc into the CD tray of the computer. As Jonathan waits for the cover page to appear on the desktop, he remarks, "It takes a few minutes to load." Once the image appears, he clicks on it, then clicks again on a series of icons to get to the story he wants to read.

Once there, Jonathan moves the mouse to each icon and, without clicking, listens to a voice explain the choice represented by the icon. One button allows Jonathan to have difficult vocabulary highlighted in the text, another button allows him to click on a word in the text and have it read to him, another allows him to have the entire text read to him, and a fourth allows him to choose animated illustration versus standard illustration. Jonathan turns on the software features allowing individual words to be read when clicked on and highlighting difficult vocabulary. He also turns on the animation feature, "just for fun," he says. He reads each page of the story, clicking on some of the difficult words, which are highlighted in blue, to have definitions read aloud to him. Jonathan clicks on other words in the text to have them read to him. For the most part, he reads independently, giggling at some of the animated illustrations and making evaluative comments such as "I don't know why that word is highlighted. *Hollow* isn't a hard word. It means empty."

———

According to his teacher, Jonathan loves books. He regularly checks them out of his school library, anxiously awaits the whole-class read-aloud each day, writes his own stories using a combination of invented spelling and the conventional spellings that he is mastering, and is growing into an independent reader. Our observation reveals that Jonathan's mastery of literacy extends beyond the printed page. He is comfortable and capable with navigating a piece of software, uses vocabulary associated with new literacies (e.g., *loading*) and utilizes features of electronic text to enhance his reading experience, such as learning the meaning of a new word at the exact moment that meaning will aid in comprehension. Even with a relatively simple narrative text at the primary-grade level, it is clear that electronic text requires new skills and strategies on the part of the reader.

Now consider the features of the Internet. Perhaps the most important reading skills that children need now, and they did not need even 10 years ago, are those associated with the Internet. Students need to know how to search for information on the Internet. They need to know how to make decisions about which websites to visit based on the results of their searches. Once they get to a website, they need to learn how to move within it—how to decide which links to click on, how to move backward and forward within the site, and how to save important pages. As they collect information, students will need the critical thinking skills necessary to evaluate the likely credibility of the information, the ability to compare and contrast multiple sources of information, and the ability to synthesize information across sources.

What we've just described exemplifies many of the concepts we address in this chapter, which is devoted to the instructional *content* needed to create competent readers and writers in the digital age in conjunction with the instructional *practices* that are related to effective literacy–technology integration. In essence, this chapter is framed by three questions:

1. What strategies for reading and communication are needed to achieve full literacy in the digital information age? In other words, *what should be taught*?

2. What instructional methods are required in the digital information age? In other words, *how can students be supported in the acquisition of these strategies*?

3. What instructional methods are facilitated by the digital information age? In other words, *what new possibilities are offered by technology to support and extend instruction*?

We address these topics within three major sections:

➤ Reading Competencies for the Digital Information Age

➤ Communication Competencies for the Digital Information Age

➤ Best Practices for Digital Literacy Development

READING COMPETENCIES
FOR THE DIGITAL INFORMATION AGE

While word recognition competence is no less important to reading online documents than it is to reading paper documents, it is the nature of *comprehension* that seems to differ most with electronic text as compared to print material. Children like Jonathan will likely bring the strong comprehension skills they are developing with print text to their reading of electronic text, but for students who struggle to make sense of print text, electronic text can be daunting (Coiro, 2005b). As Coiro (2003) articulates, the way information is presented on the Internet both allows for and requires different kinds of processing and meaning making than students and teachers are accustomed to: "Web-based texts are typically nonlinear, interactive, and inclusive of multiple media forms. Each of these characteristics affords new opportunities while also presenting a range of challenges that require new thought processes for making meaning" (p. 459).

It is a unique challenge both to understand the text in front of you, which may include graphic features such as changes in font size and color, icons, photographs, animation, video clips, and even advertisements, and to make decisions about what text will appear before you next.

> ➢ Will you scroll down the webpage until you reach the end?
> ➢ Will you click on one of the words or icons designed to take you to another location?
> ➢ If you choose to click, can you infer which links are likely to provide you with the information you wish to get?
> ➢ Which link will you click on first and why?

These decisions illustrate the complexity of "reading" the Internet. Literal or surface-level comprehension gives way to more productive and demanding higher-order thinking. Fortunately, in the last 30 years, we have amassed a great deal of information about skills and strategies needed for text comprehension (Pearson, Roehler, Dole, & Duffy, 1992; Pressley, 2000). Recent research has focused on what highly skilled readers do to understand text, and comprehension research is beginning to address the unique features of digital text (Coiro, 2005c; Duke & Pearson, 2002; Kymes, 2005; Pressley, 2000; Pressley & Afflerbach, 1995; Schmar-Dobler, 2003). The comprehension strategies listed in Figure 5.1 include some that have been recognized for a number of years and more recent additions based on research with highly skilled readers. These strategies take on a heightened sense of importance and become more nuanced when reading electronic text, particularly online text.

One of the paradoxes of reading on the Internet is that students can access multiple texts in a matter of seconds with nothing more than the click of a mouse,

- Setting Purposes for Reading
- Asking and Answering Questions
- Examining Text Structure
- Making Predictions
- Making Inferences
- Integrating New Ideas with Prior Knowledge
- Creating Images and Visual Representations
- Determining What Is Important
- Skimming, Scanning, and Selective Reading
- Summarizing and Synthesizing
- Dealing with Graphic Information
- Monitoring and Repairing Comprehension
- Interpreting and Evaluating Information
- Navigating Text

FIGURE 5.1. Fourteen strategies for comprehending text used by skilled readers.

yet the higher-level processing required to make sense of the information is more complex, not less, than with conventional print. Citing Tapscott (1998), Coiro (2003) indicates, "It's not just point and click. It's point, read, think, click" (p. 459).

It is clear that as we step further into the digital age, the comprehension strategies used by skilled readers must be the comprehension strategies used by *all* readers. These higher-level comprehension strategies need to be developed throughout the elementary school years, beginning in the primary grades (Leu, Leu, & Coiro, 2004). We now take a closer look at each of the comprehension strategies we've mentioned within the context of the Internet and other information and communication technologies (ICTs).

Comprehension Strategies

In this section, we describe each of the 14 comprehension strategies with an eye toward the Internet and other ICTs. Although we discuss each strategy individually, they work in concert. For example, students can ask and answer questions to help guide their purpose for reading and also to monitor their comprehension as they read. Similarly, it is impossible to summarize without also determining what is important, which in turn is related to setting purposes for reading.

In addition to using comprehension strategies in an integrated manner, good readers use them efficiently. That is, they employ strategies as needed, bearing in mind that strategy use is influenced by factors such as type of text, purpose for reading, level of prior knowledge related to text content and structure, and personal interest in the topic. When good readers know a great deal about the topic, they may choose to scan the text for what they don't know rather than engaging in deep reading. Similarly, the way they engage in the pleasure reading of a magazine article will likely differ from the way in which they read a textbook chapter on which they will be quizzed.

Here is a brief description of each comprehension strategy listed in Figure 5.1.

➤ *Setting Purposes for Reading.* Because of the sheer volume of information available, the rapidity with which it can be made to appear on the screen, and the potential for distracting the reader from his or her initial purpose, it is vital to teach students how to be clear about why they are reading what they are and how to monitor continually what they are reading to be sure it is aligned with their purpose.

➤ *Asking and Answering Questions.* This strategy is a strong comprehension tool for monitoring and assessing ongoing understanding. With respect to the Internet, questioning can help students think through the likely credibility of an information source and provide a foundation for searching with questions and key words.

➤ *Examining Text Structure.* The inclusion of new text features such as hyperlinks, animated graphics, pull-down menus, and site-specific search windows has changed the nature of text structure. Becoming aware of the general text features of the Internet, as well as site-specific text features that may change on a regular basis, presents a new comprehension challenge.

➤ *Making Predictions.* Students are typically taught to make predictions about what they may find in upcoming text based on illustrations, text they've already read, and headings. Now, they will also make predictions based on the names of websites and links within websites to decide what to click and when to click it.

➤ *Making Inferences.* Inferring, the ability to understand what has not been stated directly in the text, requires combining pieces of information that are provided in the text but not necessarily together and/or combining information found in the text with prior knowledge. Online text expands the scope of inferring to include skills such as determining the potential usefulness of a website and the types of information likely to be found by clicking on certain links, which can also be related to the interpretation and evaluation of online information.

➤ *Integrating New Ideas with Prior Knowledge.* Now, in addition to recalling what is already known about a topic, readers must recall what is known about various webpages and search mechanisms. Since website design features are highly variable and constantly changing, even a known website may look different tomorrow than it did today. It is important to use prior knowledge to make predictions about upcoming reading and to adjust and extend prior knowledge as new information is encountered.

➤ *Creating Images and Visual Representations.* Visualizing while reading and creating mental images of ideas represented in text or stories as they unfold take on a new dimension with the inclusion of graphics in many electronic texts. These graphics can enhance or compete with readers' visual representations.

➤ *Determining What Is Important.* This mental process may begin before any text is called up on the screen, with the construction of a key word or words to guide a search. Throughout the process of navigating the Web and reading text, students are required to focus on this aspect of comprehension, a task that can be difficult given the wide variety of information available and the bias and/or commercial intent underlying many information sources.

➤ *Skimming, Scanning, and Selective Reading.* Many researchers believe that the volume of text available on the Internet requires readers to engage more fully in skimming, scanning, and selective reading than they have in the past. Indeed, these strategies may now be an integral part of the reading process.

➤ *Summarizing and Synthesizing.* Again, the volume of text on the Internet requires almost constant comparison of information across multiple sources. Additionally, it is important for readers regularly to stop and be sure they can put into their own words what it is they are reading.

➤ *Dealing with Graphic Information.* As indicated previously, learning how to read in a multimedia environment where information may be conveyed through virtual tours, photos, and the like, takes the interpretation of graphic information to a new level of importance.

➤ *Monitoring and Repairing Comprehension.* Self-regulation becomes more important than ever, not only in the mental processes associated with comprehension, but also in the processing associated with navigation—moving strategically within and among websites.

➤ *Interpreting and Evaluating Information.* Since posting information online is not regulated, students cannot assume that because it is in the public domain, it is true, accurate, and credible. Leu, Leu, and Coiro (2004) provide a wealth of information about conducting searches as well as an easy-to-remember way of helping children become critical consumers in the information world. They suggest helping students apply the familiar questions who, what, when, where, why, and how to information they locate online. Specific questions are provided in Figure 5.2. Guiding students through these questions with increasing depth over time and showing them how to locate answers is a powerful way of teaching critical literacy skills that can transfer across the curriculum and the grades.

➤ *Navigating Text.* To some degree, this strategy encompasses all the others, especially Skimming, Scanning, and Selective Reading. In recent years, the term *navigating* has come to be associated with the Internet, and it requires knowing the difference between browsing and searching and when to use each, how to move within and

- WHO created the information at this site?
  - Can you determine the person or the unit that created this site?
  - What is the background of the creator?
  - Is this a commercial (.com), organizational (.org), or an educational (.edu) location?
- WHAT is the purpose of this site?
  - Can you locate a link that tells you what this site is about? What does it say the purpose of the site is? How confident can you be that this is a fair statement?
  - Knowing who created the site, can you infer why they created it?
- WHEN was the information at this site created?
  - How recently was the information at this site updated?
  - Is it likely this information has changed since it appeared? How? Why?
- WHERE can I go to check the accuracy of this information?
  - Are the sources for factual information clearly listed so I can check them with another source?
  - If not, how confident can you be in the information at this location?
  - Does the information provided at this site match up with facts located at another website about the topic?
- WHY did this person, or group, put this information on the Internet?
  - What is this person, or group, trying to accomplish with the information they provide?
  - How can you tell?
- HOW is the information at this site shaped by the stance taken by the creator of the site?
  - Knowing who created this site and what the stated or implicit purpose is, how does this probably shape the information or the activities here?
  - What biases are likely to appear at this location?

FIGURE 5.2. Questions to guide the evaluation of online information. From Leu, Leu, and Coiro (2004). Copyright 2004 by Christopher-Gordon. Reprinted by permission.

among websites, and how to save important webpages. It also includes the ability to get to the information sources best suited to the reader's purpose as efficiently as possible—knowing when to stop and linger and when to move on quickly.

Before discussing instructional approaches, we want to emphasize the importance of beginning comprehension instruction as early as kindergarten and continuing it into high school (Pressley & Block, 2002). Children in kindergarten benefit from teacher modeling and think-alouds, as they actively construct meaning from books they hear read to them and books they are learning to read independently. Time spent building listening comprehension skills is a worthwhile investment in later reading comprehension. Children in middle school and high school benefit from instruction in comprehension of a wider range of text types and for a wider range of purposes, including studying and test taking.

Instructional Approaches

Duke and Pearson (2002) suggest that comprehension instruction should include a balance between explicit instruction in specific comprehension strategies and time for students to engage in actual reading, writing, and discussion of text. It is important to provide students time to read text at both their instructional and independent levels, thus promoting practice and mastery in applying new skills and strategies to a wide range of texts. Coupled with comprehension instruction, this strategy encourages the development of independent readers.

Reading and Researching with the Internet in Laura's Third-Grade Classroom

It is a crisp day in November and the students in Laura's third-grade class are seated at their computers in the computer lab. The purpose for their time in the lab is to find information about the Native American tribes they are studying, specifically their styles of houses. Students are also expected to analyze why the styles varied from those in the Northwest Coastal region. After Laura has modeled how to find the bookmarked websites and navigate within them, she discusses the importance of carefully examining the information provided. During a think-aloud, Laura points out the author of each website, the organization sponsoring the site, and the copyright date. She shares her expectation that students will engage in an evaluation plan, using the checklist she provides for them, as they explore the designated sites for their research. As students work on the task, Laura moves among them, assisting when needed and monitoring their progress. As necessary, she directs students to explore websites that are perhaps better suited for their needs. Students work respectfully and collaboratively to support each other as they locate and examine the needed information. In the process, they eagerly read the information they are locating online while Laura periodically asks questions to check comprehension. The following day, students pick up where they left off, and in the days that follow they actively engage in note taking, comparing, and contrasting, eventually presenting their findings in a PowerPoint report that includes text and pictures.

In Laura's classroom, we see several dimensions that characterize the effective integration of technology into literacy instruction. Laura's students are learning the new literacy skills of navigating websites, reading electronic text, and evaluating website credibility in conjunction with the traditional literacy skills associated with reading to learn and doing research. Laura first models what she wants them to do, using a think-aloud to make explicit her decisions and how she is making them. She then supports her students with a checklist to guide them through their practice and monitors their progress, providing assistance when needed.

Laura's monitoring for understanding, or in-the-moment assessment, leads her to adjust her teaching plan so that students who are struggling to read the websites can be successful with websites at their reading levels. In other words, she differentiates instruction based on her students' individual needs. The work process itself is marked by academic talk among students, who work together to solve problems. Today's class is part of a longer unit of study, allowing students time for in-depth learning and understanding. It is also a unit in which content-area study and literacy development are integrally linked.

Laura's instruction reflects much of what is found in the five-step model of comprehension instruction described by Duke and Pearson (2002, pp. 208–209):

1. Explicit description of the strategy and when and how it should be used
2. Teacher and/or student modeling of the strategy in action
3. Collaborative use of the strategy in action
4. Guided practice using the strategy with gradual release of responsibility
5. Independent use of the strategy

While these steps are easy to remember and extremely powerful instructional tools, they require an investment of time on the part of both teachers and students. Pressley (2000) describes comprehension strategy development as "a long-term developmental process" (p. 551). The five steps listed above are meant to extend over enough time—usually a period of several weeks or more—to ensure that students reach the independent stage, marked by their ability to determine on their own when the strategy is needed and to put it into action without teacher prodding. In order to explain more fully how this model of comprehension instruction can work in your classroom, we elaborate each step below.

Step 1: Explicitly Describe the Strategy and When and How to Use It

An important and often neglected part of this step involves explaining to students both *how* and *when* to use the strategy. Laura's instructional activity engages students in the active use of multiple comprehension strategies. They are reading to learn about the types of houses occupied by various Native American tribes. Thus, they are challenged to keep purpose for reading in the forefront as they sift through information on two or three websites. The two main strategies they are practicing are skimming, scanning, and selective reading and summarizing and synthesizing. These strategies are not new to Laura's students; they have been working with them at varying levels of independence for several weeks. Laura uses language like the following to state directly what they are learning and why:

> LAURA: You've been working on your reports on your Native American tribes and you've checked a number of books for information. Now you're going to have a chance to check some sources on the Internet to add to the information you've collected. You will visit at least one website today, maybe two or three. When you get there, your job is to search the site for information about the type of home, also called a dwelling, that your

Native American tribe might have lived in many years ago or perhaps still lives in today. Do you think you'll be able to find that information when you check your websites?

(*Several hands shoot up and Laura selects Shanda.*)

SHANDA: Yes.

LAURA: Do you think that's the only information that will be on your website? Or do you think there will be other information on the site?

Most of the students agree that their websites are likely to contain a great deal more than just information about homes, and Laura uses this response to segue into her next point:

Yes, websites usually have a lot of information on them. So it will be very important for you to use your skimming and scanning skills to decide where you're going to find the information you need and then to focus your attention on those sections.

Continuing with a question-and-answer format, she reviews with the students what skimming and scanning are, then explains summarizing and synthesizing. Because this is a review, rather than an introduction of the strategies, this exchange is brief, leading quickly into the next step.

Step 2: Model the Strategy in Action

Laura models strategy use by calling attention to the website she has up on her laptop projected onto a screen at the front of the computer lab. As she navigates the site, she describes what she is doing with the mouse and what she is thinking as she does it. She tells students which parts of the text she is skimming, what she is picking up from skimming and scanning, and how she decides what to read in more detail. She then has students help her read a small portion and asks them to help her think aloud about what they are learning and where they can record the information on their note-taking sheet, a learning guide that Laura and the technology specialist designed specifically for this lesson.

Step 3: Practice the Strategy in Collaboration with Others

After modeling and thinking aloud, Laura takes all of her students to the same webpage and encourages them to work together on the examination of the information there, providing them an opportunity to seek support from peers as they skim, scan, summarize, and synthesize. Laura observes which students are working independently and provides scaffolded support to those who need it.

Step 4: Use the Strategy with Gradual Release of Responsibility

Students are working independently, assisted by their learning guide. Although they are not formally working together, they do ask one another for help, as needed.

Step 5: Use the Strategy Independently

Laura engages in the five-step model of comprehension instruction with the intent that her students will be able independently to apply skimming, scanning, summarizing, and synthesizing to reading multiple websites by the end of the school year. While some students are already at that point, Laura has a research project planned for the spring that will enable all of them to demonstrate their proficiency. In the meantime, she uses this project to continue to teach skimming, scanning, summarizing, and synthesizing while simultaneously laying a foundation for later work focusing on how to evaluate websites critically. At the bottom of their note-taking sheet, students list the creator of the website, when the information was last updated, and the name of one person or information source that serves to validate the credibility of the site. As student proficiency with skimming, scanning, summarizing, and synthesizing increases, Laura will move website evaluation to the forefront.

As we write this book, comprehension strategy research is on the edge of an exciting frontier—the emergence of work focused on the processes readers use to comprehend electronic text. We encourage you to take the information we've provided here as a starting point and to build on it based on your own observations of children as you develop instruction designed to meet the needs of your students.

New Possibilities with Technology

While the Internet poses many challenges to traditional notions of reading comprehension, it also offers new possibilities. As indicated in the report of the National Reading Panel (2000), mastery of sight words, automatic decoding skills, and the development of a rich and extensive vocabulary are essential to independent text comprehension. The development of word recognition strategies such as phonic analysis and sight word development are central to primary-grade literacy instruction and may continue into the middle and upper elementary grades, especially for English language learners and struggling readers.

In this regard, there are two ways to optimize your integration of technology into the classroom. First, technology can assist students who have not yet mastered the word recognition strategies or vocabulary needed to participate in other literacy events, such as comprehension strategy development or writing development, opening the door to participation. Second, technology can assist you in accelerating growth in word recognition and vocabulary. The National Reading Panel (2000) stated that electronic text accompanied by speech and hypertext (specifically, highlighted text linked to important definitions or supporting text) holds promise for reading development. Additionally, the wider access to information about low-readability text (i.e., text with grade-appropriate themes and content that is comprehensible to students reading below grade level) through online sources may help teachers to provide students with greater opportunities for independent practice in both silent and oral reading formats.

Finally, word processing and multimedia software expand the possibilities for meaning making in children of all ages. Since reading instruction is most effective when combined with writing instruction (National Reading Panel, 2000), tools that support writing development simultaneously support reading development. We now turn our attention to the development of communication competencies for the digital information age.

COMMUNICATION COMPETENCIES FOR THE DIGITAL INFORMATION AGE

Communication in the 21st century is rapidly changing. It used to be that word processing was the equivalent of typing a paper; we did not go to the computer until we had worked through several drafts by hand. Now, each step of the writing process can be completed electronically, from brainstorming to rough drafts to final paper ready for publication. Word processing programs now routinely include templates for various types of written communication, and presentation software makes it possible to combine text and graphics to convey information in ways that were beyond most of our imaginations 20 years ago; today their use can be expected of even elementary school students. In today's world, methods of communication include e-mail, instant messaging, text messaging, weblogs, chat rooms, web-based video conferencing, websites, and electronic bulletin boards (Leu, Leu, & Coiro, 2004).

Creating Newspapers in Darin's Third-, Fourth-, and Fifth-Grade Classroom

It is February, and Darin's students have been learning about newspapers and writing articles to be included in newspapers they are creating in small groups. Prior to this lesson, they have worked together in small groups to research topics, conduct interviews, plan, and write. It is time for the students to begin the process of taking their notes and handwritten copy to their laptops and learning how to format it like a newspaper.

Using his laptop and a projection system, Darin demonstrates the mechanics of saving several files together so that individual articles can appear in the same newspaper. He then shows ways of formatting articles in a newspaper style, including setting up columns, reducing margin size to allow for more text, and moving captions without affecting columns. This demonstration is interactive, and Darin involves his students in generating ideas for accomplishing the various tasks. "How do you think we can get the title of this article centered above the article?" he asks. The students call out suggestions and debate the pros and cons of various approaches.

Throughout this lesson, Darin discusses a variety of visual features of newspapers and presents examples of how students might incorporate these features in their own newspapers. When it comes to pictures, Darin engages his students in an important discussion about using clip art. "What do you think about including clip art?" he asks the class. The students want to include this visual feature in their newspapers, suggesting that they can find some online. Darin agrees to the use of clip art but reminds them that he was dissatisfied with its use in several of their PowerPoint presentations. "There was too much emphasis on moving text and clip art and not enough emphasis on content," he explains. "I want you to do just the opposite in this assignment. Spend more time on content and less time on clip art."

Darin brings the lesson to a close with a reminder to give all group members an opportunity for input. He then directs one member of each group to distribute laptops. The resulting group newspapers vary in content, including articles about recent movies, spring fashion trends, and results of interviews with building staff. Each newspaper is proudly presented to peers and the school community.

A snapshot of Darin's students at work reveals how these writers prepare articles designed to engage and inform their audience. Their readers learn about locally occurring events such as school spirit week and those occurring at the international level, including the Olympic Games. They are entertained as they read riddles and complete crossword puzzles. They are persuaded to consider reading books, based on compelling reviews. They are informed of upcoming weather patterns, perspectives held by school personnel on various topics, and the meanings of vocabulary words such as *quetzal* (a brightly colored bird found in Central and South America, in case you are wondering).

Writing and the Writing Process

Writing, one of the most frequently used modes of communication, is used to inspire, entertain, persuade, and inform. Toward these ends, writers present their work in many different ways depending upon their purpose and audience. Technology widens the range of options available for written communication, both at the levels of process and product.

In the creation of newspapers, Darin's students move seamlessly between conventional and electronic communication formats. During the *prewriting* phase, students work with pencil and paper. They then use their notes to create *drafts* of their articles with voice—making personal connections to the gathered information. Next, Darin models how to make their work print-ready with the support of technology. They word-process their drafts and *revise* their articles based on self-assessment and feedback from peers; additions and deletions are made using the cut and paste features of word processing software. They also use spell check as part, though not all, of the *editing* process.

To promote ease of reading, students carefully position text. To capture and hold the attention of their audience, they use various fonts and font sizes. Clip art is found online and used to support the message of the text; this visual form of communication also serves to advance the reader's thinking. The inclusion of a newspaper title, an editorial note, and contributors' names and roles, including chief editor and reporter, reflects student understanding of a newspaper and its components. At the point of *publication*, Darin and his students celebrate their work. They are proud of their collaborative effort and are pleased to share it with visitors perusing student work on display in the halls of their elementary school.

Depth and Breadth of the Lesson Progression

Throughout his instruction, Darin promotes student understanding of the collective importance of content, layout, and design of a newspaper. He provides an opportunity for students to engage in wide reading from various genres, utilize comprehension strategies, use written language and graphics to communicate effectively in the newspaper style, and apply their knowledge of language structure and conventions to the final copy. Darin also creatively moves students from conventional literacy to electronic literacy, encouraging them to capitalize on the best of both.

In addition, Darin addresses one of the challenges of new technology: the ease with which students can take the words of others and use them as their own. As students engage in online searches for information to report in their articles, he reminds them to take original notes rather than cutting and pasting text. Coiro (2005b) captures this issue in the question "How do I synthesize without copying?" (p. 34) and has created a graphic organizer to help students make information their own (see Figure 5.3).

Instructional Approaches

Darin uses several of the same instructional approaches that Laura uses as she guides her students through a research unit. Here, we highlight those that are pivotal. First, he models for students with a think-aloud how to save files together and format articles in newspaper style. Second, he uses information gleaned from his observations of previous student work to shape his instruction by explicitly sharing his expectation that students focus on content rather than clip art. Third, he engages students in guided practice as they move from whole-group instruction to their smaller groups. Fourth, he carefully monitors students as they prepare their newspapers. In the end, students are able to apply what they learn from Darin during the instructional phase of the lesson to the guided practice and independent phases—the ultimate goal of all instruction.

New Possibilities with Technology

Word processing software enables the rapid creation and formatting of newsletters, newspapers, flyers, lists, and letters. Another tool for communication is multimedia presentation software such as PowerPoint, for use by teachers and students to deliver information in an appealing manner. The features of this software include text, pictorials, speech, sound effects, and motion. Together, these aspects promote creativity in the presentation of information and contribute to active engagement on the part of the audience. When students use multimedia presentation software,

Paste into this graphic organizer segments of text relevant to your research question. Then record your summary of and reactions to the text.

My research question is: _____

_____

Source(s): Copy and paste text or image source here and provide URL for each source.

a. Summary: The most salient points of the text are:

_____

b. Personal connection: This information connects to other information I have found in the following ways:

_____

This information changes my thinking in the following ways:

_____

My original synthesis, which considers significant points from my sources, is:

_____

My supporting statements, informed by at least two of my summaries and at least two of my personal connection statements, are:

_____

FIGURE 5.3. How to synthesize online sources. From Coiro (2005b). Copyright 2005 by Association for Supervision and Curriculum Development. Reprinted by permission. The Association for Supervision and Curriculum Development is a worldwide community of educators advocating sound policies and sharing best practices to achieve the success of each learner. To learn more, visit ASCD at *www.ascd.org*.

they are encouraged to make thoughtful decisions about how best to organize information, which design elements (e.g., animation, sound effects) and media most effectively convey their message, how to document resources, and how they will move within the presentation.

In addition, teachers can use presentation software to enhance their instruction. For example, Leia, like Laura, engages her students in a social studies unit on Northwest Coastal Indians. Her instruction includes a PowerPoint presentation featuring photographs of totem poles and the ways in which families created them to represent the history and legends of specific tribes.

The use of e-mail opens the gate to communication with others anywhere and at any time. One very popular project involving e-mail is the Flat Stanley project, developed by classroom teacher Dale Hubert and inspired by the children's book *Flat Stanley* (Brown & Bjorkman, 1964). As Hubert (2005) explains, this WebQuest provides learners an opportunity to send Stanley (a boy flattened as a result of a falling bulletin board) in hard copy or electronic form to another place, near or far. While Stanley is away, he engages in adventures and records, with the help of his host, details of those adventures. Upon Stanley's return home, via mail or email, students are pleased to learn where he's been. So far, he's been at the White House, in the space shuttle, and to many other places of interest all around the world. Involvement in a project such as Flat Stanley provides students an opportunity to engage collaboratively in conventional and new literacies while making cross-curricular connections.

Finally, new technologies have tremendous potential for emergent literacy development. Word processing and multimedia software encourage young children to make meaning using a variety of symbols and forms. According to Labbo and Kuhn (1998, p. 83), studies of kindergarteners reveal that young children who engage with computers develop concepts about electronic symbol making; for example:

> Computers are used to accomplish personal and public communicative goals.

> Computers are repositories of symbols and symbol-making tools.

> Computers are used for playing, creating art, composing, printing, and publishing.

> Meaning making may take a variety of multimedia and symbolic forms.

Leu, Leu, and Coiro (2004) suggest that the new literacies of the Internet and other ICTs revolve around five core processes related to gathering and disseminating information: "*identifying* important questions, *navigating* information networks to locate relevant information, *critically evaluating* information, *synthesizing* information, and *communicating* the solutions to others" (p. 132). Developing readers, writers, and thinkers for the 21st century means developing in children not only the skills and strategies to enable these higher-level cognitive processes, but also positive dispositions toward new technologies (Castek, Bevans-Mangleson, & Goldstone, 2006; Leu, Kinzer, Coiro, & Cammack, 2004).

BEST PRACTICES FOR DIGITAL LITERACY DEVELOPMENT

In Chapter 2, we outlined research-based best practices for literacy development. Here, we want to emphasize five dimensions of best practices that are central to strong literacy–technology integration: the classroom as a learning community; connections among reading, writing, and talking; connecting literacy and content-area instruction; meeting individual student needs; and the teacher as active decision maker.

The Classroom as a Learning Community

We cannot say often enough how important it is to establish a community of learners in your classroom. Constructive social interaction and productive classroom talk should be as central to the curriculum as the content being taught. In classrooms where literacy and technology are effectively integrated, teachers are attentive to grouping strategies and classroom management techniques that build, maintain, and enhance the learning circle.

Connections among Reading, Writing, and Talking

In a recent study, Allington and Johnston (2002) found classroom talk to be a central component in the classrooms of exemplary teachers. Specifically, they found that these teachers expected, modeled, and taught productive ways of communicating as an integral part of the learning process. They encouraged students to use talk as a means of exploring new ideas and working collaboratively. In both Laura's and Darin's classrooms, student talk is more than allowed—it is encouraged. Furthermore, both teachers use discussion as a form of instruction. Discussion is recognized as an essential component of reading and writing development in both conventional and digital formats (Duke & Pearson, 2002; McKenna, Labbo, & Reinking, 2003).

Connecting Literacy and Content-Area Instruction

Research indicates that effective teachers often use a thematic approach in order to foster in-depth learning over a substantive period of time. Allington and Johnston (2002) suggest that "integration across subjects, topics, and time fosters engagement and curricular coherence" (p. 215).

New technologies, especially the Internet, facilitate the integration of literacy instruction with content-area instruction. In addition to allowing for greater curricular coherence, technology exposes students to more informational text than ever. Duke's (2000) ground-breaking study, "3.6 Minutes Per Day: The Scarcity of Informational Text in First Grade," revealed how little preparation students get in the early grades for the relatively high informational text reading demands that emerge in third or fourth grade and continue for the remainder of the school years. This study has been a catalyst for greater emphasis on informational text beginning in kindergarten, with students engaged in reading the text themselves as well as being read to.

Meeting Individual Student Needs

Almost all of the teachers we work with echo Jon David's sentiment that technology allows for "a more level playing field" for their students, shifting the dynamics between high and low achievers, and allowing teachers to see greater possibilities for their lower-achieving students. Careful teacher observation coupled with the new possibilities afforded by technology can greatly lessen the learning burden for many students while simultaneously supporting them in the acquisition of critical literacy. Speech recognition software allows children (and adults) who struggle with the mechanics of handwriting to be writers nonetheless, and, as mentioned previously, "talking books" and other unique features of electronic text hold promise for early readers and writers, older students who struggle with reading and writing, and English language learners (McKenna, 1998).

In order for students to reap these potential benefits, it is critical that they engage in the use of technology and the development of new literacies on an equal basis with their peers. You may have noticed in the examples in this chapter that *all* students were engaged in the acquisition of new literacies and that all were actively engaged with technology.

The Teacher as Active Decision Maker

Finally, teaching effectively with technology requires active decision making on the part of the teacher. In Chapter 4, we considered the decisions teachers engage in as they prepare for instruction. In this chapter, we have explored issues related to the content and methods of instruction. In the next chapter, we address the examination of student work as a part of the assessment and instructional processes.

INQUIRY AND REFLECTION

In this chapter, we discussed comprehension strategy instruction as it relates to literacy–technology integration. You may teach comprehension strategies articulated in a reading series or district guide. Perhaps you and your building-level colleagues have coordinated efforts in teaching comprehension strategies across the grades. Perhaps you use approaches such as "know, want to know, learn" (K-W-L; Ogle, 1986), Reciprocal Teaching (Palincsar & Brown, 1986), or Question–Answer Relationships (Raphael, 1982) to address a cluster of strategies in an integrated manner.

Using the Chart for Reflecting on Comprehension Strategy Instruction in My Classroom, found in Appendix K, write a sentence or short phrase describing how and when you address each strategy using digital text in your classroom. When you have finished the chart, look at the patterns in what you've written. Record responses to the following questions in your anecdotal log:

> ➢ Which strategies get the most attention in your classroom? Are there strategies that you do not address at all?

> ➢ What is your rationale for the strategies you do address and those you don't?

> ➢ What changes might you make in how technology is embedded within your comprehension strategy instruction? How do you plan to begin?

CHAPTER 6

USING ASSESSMENT TO INFORM DECISION MAKING IN THE TECHNOLOGY-ENRICHED LEARNING ENVIRONMENT

Using Technology to Support Content-Area Literacy in Leia's Fifth-Grade Classroom

Leia is making plans to engage her students in a 2-week unit of study focusing on Abraham Lincoln and the Civil War. She develops the unit to increase students' knowledge of specific aspects related to this time period, which they then share with peers and visitors to their elementary school. She weaves technology into the lesson progression. It will serve as a resource for student research, an organizational tool for report development, and a means for publication. Other components of the planning phase are the development of a graphic organizer, the creation of a student checklist to record progress, and the development of a rubric for Leia to use as she follows student performance.

Leia designs this unit to align with historical nonfiction presented in the district reading series. At the onset of the unit, Leia and the media technology specialist at her school share with students how to record findings from their online search in their own words. Then each student is ready to research online one of the following areas: Abraham Lincoln's early life, Abraham Lincoln's political life and assassination, the Civil War, and the Battle of Gettysburg and the Gettysburg Address, with plans to contribute their individually completed work to that of their team. Once students collect their research, they meet with others examining the same topic to confirm their findings. Leia and the media technology specialist model for students how to use software to develop an outline for their reports in the form of a concept map. A template for this outline provides a scaffold for students who are less familiar with this task. Once students have revised their drafts of the reports and published them using a word processing program, they meet with team members to complete posters, which include a title, each of the sections they researched, and pictures found on the Internet. Then students present their report on the poster to their peers.

Throughout the implementation of the unit, students keep track of their progress using a checklist; Leia uses a rubric to guide her assessment of students' level of proficiency with concept map development, contribution to the group poster, pictures, and presentation. All in all, the lesson provides meaningful learning opportunities with content-area connections to literacy supported by technology.

Throughout this unit, Leia gathers information from students to determine the level at which they are learning or performing the assigned tasks. This information informs her decision making regarding present and future instructional plans. In some instances, Leia decides that the best plan is to reteach content, either to a small group or to the whole class, using another instructional approach. At other times, she decides that the best plan is to move forward. During each of the lessons in this unit, Leia and her students actively monitor their progress. At the beginning of the unit, Leia discusses with students her expectations for quality work and the rationale behind the expectations; more specifically, they consider what quality work looks like. As the unit unfolds, Leia and her students dialogue about Leia's observations of their work and the students' own perceptions of their work, as articulated on a self-assessment form, with the goal of increasing success during the remaining stages of the project. As the learning opportunity comes to a close, Leia and her students use the criteria presented earlier to determine the degree to which they have achieved the objectives. This information helps Leia make decisions about future instruction.

Leia's lesson progression is one example of the way literacy assessment in the 21st century has changed. Rather than depending solely on traditional assessments, such as individually administered, paper-and-pencil, short-answer tests, to learn what students understand about Abraham Lincoln and the Civil War, Leia engages her students in meaningful assessment opportunities designed to inform her instruction. This assessment plan suggests an emphasis on higher-order thinking in conjunction with the acquisition of important historical facts. In Leia's classroom, where a constructivist approach to learning is promoted, assessment is embedded in instruction.

This chapter focuses on meaningful assessment components of literacy–technology integration. We begin by addressing the purposes of assessment, discussing approaches to examining student work, and addressing the role of students in the assessment process. Then we consider how assessment affects the phases of the instructional cycle. Next we explore the potential of technology to affect the assessment process, and finally we discuss reflective practice, which is at the heart of meaningful instruction.

PURPOSES OF ASSESSMENT

As described by McTighe and O'Connor (2005), there are three major categories of assessment: summative, diagnostic, and formative. The purpose of specific assessments determines their placement within these categories. *Summative* assessment, which is frequently evaluative and characterized by a grade or score, offers a summary of learning that has resulted from engagement in a unit of study. Specific examples of this type of assessment include final exams, tests, culminating projects, and work portfolios. *Diagnostic* assessment, often a precursor to instruction, can be designed to reveal students' background knowledge, level of skill development, misunderstandings, interests, and learning styles. The outcome of diagnostic assessment is not translated into a grade. *Formative* assessment, including teacher observation, review of student work, student response to questions, and learner engagement in think-alouds, occurs as instruction is delivered; its purpose is to provide direction for instruction. Although teachers may record student outcomes to these assessments, they are not intended to contribute to a final grade.

Graves and colleagues (2004) provide another useful way to think about assessment, suggesting three related themes: assessment as inquiry, development, and measurement of progress. *Assessment as inquiry* suggests that teachers assume the role of researcher in the assessment process, developing scenarios that encourage student learning and suggest a place to begin instruction. It is important that teachers modify assessment to account for students' vast differences in individual *development*, even within a grade. Teachers use various sources of data to monitor student growth and ultimately report *measurement of progress*.

Having discussed summative, diagnostic, and formative assessment as well as assessment as inquiry, development, and measurement of progress, we now consider the role of the seven practices of effective learning delineated by McTighe and O'Connor (2005). These practices, presented in Figure 6.1, are designed to elevate learning and teaching.

Based on our work with teachers and their students, we have witnessed the potential of these practices to affect student learning. Perhaps most important, their presence can enhance motivation (Marzano, 1992). This is most likely to occur when three conditions are in place. First, students have a clear understanding of learning objectives and are aware of how teachers will monitor what has been learned. Second, students believe that learning objectives and assessments have merit and are worth the effort. Third, students believe they can effectively learn and satisfy the expectations for evaluation.

In the next section, we more closely examine assessment methods, including interest inventories, observation, process interviews, and portfolios.

Approaches to Examining Students at Work

The review of student work has great potential to reveal dimensions of learning and achievement (Sheingold & Frederiksen, 2000). Dialogue between various par-

- Practice 1: Use summative assessments to frame meaningful performance goals.
- Practice 2: Show criteria and models in advance.
- Practice 3: Assess before teaching.
- Practice 4: Offer appropriate choices.
- Practice 5: Provide feedback early and often.
- Practice 6: Encourage self-assessment and goal setting.
- Practice 7: Allow new evidence of achievement to replace old evidence.

FIGURE 6.1. Seven practices for effective learning. Based on McTighe and O'Connor (2005).

ties, including student with teacher and teacher with teacher, can lead to an understanding of what constitutes quality student work. For example, as teachers and students look at strong and weak examples of work, they both are better informed of expectations for high-quality work. A similar dialogue between teacher and teacher—in professional development study groups conducted locally or nationally or through online professional development opportunities—can also clarify criteria for successful work completion.

Interest Inventory

Interest inventories provide an inside view of students' interests. As teachers use this information during the planning phase of instruction, they can thoughtfully develop learning opportunities that are of interest to children and may motivate them to reach and even extend their potential. Teachers can become familiar with students' interests in various ways. As you may recall from Chapter 4, Jon David learns of his students' interests through their entries in the All About Me book completed at the beginning of the school year. Another way you can become familiar with interests is by having students complete an interest inventory such as the one shown in Figure 6.2.

Observation

A teacher's knowledge of student understanding can be significantly increased by observing students in action. Observation allows teachers to discover patterns that reveal student strengths and areas in need of development. This in-the-moment assessment provides information that guides both short- and long-term instructional decision making. Additionally, it can be used as feedback to students, helping them better understand their learning and offering suggestions for further growth; parents, administrators, and support staff can benefit from knowledge gained through observation in much the same way. Frequently, teachers record anecdotal notes based on what is observed as a means for monitoring student

1. What do you like most about school?

   Why is this particularly interesting to you?

2. What do you like to do in your spare time?

   Why?

3. What are three of your favorite books?

   Why did you choose these as your favorites?

4. If you could have unlimited access to technology hardware and software, what would you choose?

   Why?

5. What are some things you know a lot about?

   How did you learn about them?

6. What are some things that you would like to know more about?

   Why?

7. If you could be anywhere, where would you be?

   Why?

8. What famous person would you like to meet?

   Why?

9. What has been your greatest personal success?

   How did you achieve this?

10. What qualities do you admire in other people?

    Why do you value these qualities?

11. What would you like to be when you grow up?

    Why?

FIGURE 6.2. Interest inventory.

growth. For example, Leia suggests at the close of the historical nonfiction unit, that James demonstrates an increased understanding of the Civil War. He effec-

tively conducts an online search, develops an outline (using software), prepares his section for the group report, and presents it to his peers. He displays leadership, as he completes his work early and assists other students in their work completion. James appears to be motivated by his participation in the assessment process. Based on her observation of James, Leia plans to provide additional opportunities for him to engage in the inquiry process.

Process Interviews

This type of interview provides an inside view of how a student processes information and/or uses a strategy related to reading or communication. In the following example, a teacher, Kevin, and a fifth-grade student, Dave, are engaged in a think-aloud.

> KEVIN: I noticed that you are moving among several websites regarding the Underground Railroad. What are you thinking as you carry out this electronic search?

> DAVE: Based on what you showed us in class and what we talked about, I know I need to gather information from highly regarded websites for my PowerPoint presentation. So, as I review each website, I am thinking about what we talked about in class: accuracy, currency, and authorship.

> KEVIN: Describe what is particularly difficult for you to do during this electronic search process.

> DAVE: Well, even though I'm familiar with the criteria of credible websites, it takes me longer to cross-check each site with the criteria than I would like. As I search, I stop and ask, what are the criteria for quality websites? Which specifically relate to this assignment? I would like to be faster with evaluating a website.

> KEVIN: I understand the difficulty you're talking about. In fact, I share your goal. Do you think there are steps we can take as a class to help us be more efficient with checking for website credibility?

> DAVE: Hey! We could write down the criteria for determining accuracy, cur-

rency, and authorship on a poster and put it on a wall in the classroom, like the poster that's in the computer lab.

KEVIN: I think your suggestion to create a quick reference guide is a good idea. With your help, we can begin work on this later today.

Portfolios

The development of student portfolios is another way to follow academic growth. This assessment option allows students creatively to display and preserve selected work; most important, it provides a place for collecting evidence and representations of student learning. Students, teachers, and parents can use portfolios to reflect on strengths and areas in need of development, both in the moment and across time. Various forms of work may be included in a portfolio, both print-based and digital. For example, some entries may be handwritten, with or without an artistic component. Others may be in the form of anecdotal notes recorded by the teacher. Still others may be technology-based, featuring work on video or developed using software.

In the example shown in Figure 6.3, fourth graders Andrew and Jacob use software to present at least four ways in which they are like each other and at least

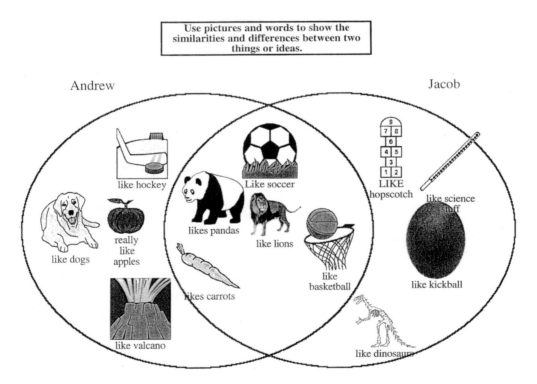

FIGURE 6.3. Fourth graders Andrew and Jacob's Venn diagram of similarities and differences.

Teacher name: Jon David   Date taught: December 11

Student name: Karen

Lesson description: After reading a PM Story Book story, students choose activities to support their learning.

Comments: Karen read the story independently, clicking only on the word *hungry* to have it pronounced by the program. She thought it might be *hurry*. Karen loved writing about the story, as indicated on the self-assessment page.

FIGURE 6.4. Second-grade teacher Jon David's comments recorded on work sample label.

four ways in which they are different from each other. From this learning opportunity, their teacher learns about their ability to compare and contrast, integrate text and graphics using technology, and gather information about their personal interests. As the teacher observes the students' task completion process, he also notes that they are highly motivated by the learning experience.

No matter the type of entry, students and/or teachers may record reflective comments to accompany it. These comments may include what has been learned, unanswered questions, and direction for future instruction. Teachers usually select work that is particularly representative of students' thinking and/or growth at a given time, often with help from students. It is useful to mount a label on the back of the selected work samples and provide the date, student name, lesson description, and comments. For example, in Figure 6.4 we learn about Karen's task and how she responded to it, based on Jon David's observations. A commentary such as Jon David's along with the work sample can be useful in parent–teacher conferences as well as in student–teacher conferences. Entries of particular interest may be those that the child is most proud of or those that challenged him or her to see the world differently.

Involving Students in the Assessment Process

It is critical that both teachers and students are familiar with the appearance of quality work and consider how to encourage its development. In keeping with this thought, Sheingold and Frederiksen (2000) recommend that assessments be "transparent," making "students and teachers keenly aware of those characteristics of outstanding performance that exemplify shared values within the community and of the reasons these characteristics are valued" (p. 325). Effective assessment represents valued student learning and aligns with the focus of instruction. Sheingold and Frederiksen explain, "Criteria and values become transparent to teachers and students, and to others who participate in the assessment system, both through materials (that is, examples, along with evaluation) and through multiple and varied opportunities to participate in the process of evaluation and reflection" (p. 326).

Reflection plays a critical role in achieving transparency. To that end, both teachers and students need to understand and appreciate characteristics of a learner's performance. It is important that they determine together what assignments promote the development and demonstration of expected characteristics. Students benefit from engaging in the assessment process, as it can promote reflection on their work in general. Specifically, engagement in the process can encourage students to consider their areas of strength and those in need of further development. Perhaps most important, the result of such engagement may be suggestions for fostering further growth. As teachers engage in the assessment process, they are challenged to consider reflectively instructional practices and ways to promote student growth aligned with what is perceived as important.

Black and Wiliam (1998) indicate that student achievement is likely to increase when teachers do the following:

➢ Make learning goals clear to students.

➢ Inform students of the ways in which their work aligns with learning goals.

➢ Engage students as partners in the assessment of learning.

➢ Provide students actions they can engage in to increase performance.

The rationale for the inclusion of students in the assessment process is strongly presented by Chappuis (2005); she suggests, "By expanding our formative assessment practices to systematically involve students as decision makers, teachers acknowledge the contributions that students make to their own success and give them the opportunity and structure they need to become active partners in improving their learning" (p. 43). Chappuis presents three assessment-related questions adapted from Atkin, Black, and Coffey (2001):

➢ *Where am I going?* In helping students understand the direction of their work, it is critical that teachers discuss with them what they are expected to accomplish, using student-friendly language and showing both exemplary and weak work examples.

➢ *Where am I now?* As a means to enhance student understanding of current levels of performance in light of what is expected, teachers provide descriptive feedback and encourage students to examine their work and develop goals.

➢ *How can I close the gap?* Students are more equipped to close the gap between where they are and where they need to be when teachers break down learning into subcomponents that students can manage, provide students time to practice revising work before it is graded, and grant students an opportunity to reflect on what they have learned.

Embedded within the three questions are seven strategies, outlined in Figure 6.5, that further articulate student engagement in the process. According to

Questions	Strategies
Where am I going?	1: Provide a clear and understandable vision of the learning target. 2: Use examples of strong and weak work.
Where am I now?	3: Offer regular descriptive feedback. 4: Teach students to self-assess and set goals.
How can I close the gap?	5: Design lessons to focus on one aspect of quality at a time. 6: Teach students focused revision. 7: Engage students in self-reflection and let them document and share their learning.

FIGURE 6.5. Questions and strategies to promote student engagement in the assessment process. From Chappuis (2005). Copyright 2005 by Association for Supervision and Curriculum Development. Reprinted by permission. The Association for Supervision and Curriculum Development is a worldwide community of educators advocating sound policies and sharing best practices to achieve the success of each learner. To learn more, visit ASCD at *www.ascd.org*.

Chappuis (2005), these strategies intend to help students gain a deeper understanding of goals, become familiar with their own skill levels in relationship to the goals, and assume responsibility for attaining the goals.

Figure 6.6 provides a means for student self-assessment and teacher feedback; it is designed in part for student and teacher to share responsibility for the assessment. Students record their perceptions of strengths and weaknesses related to their work, teachers or classmates share their perceptions, and finally, the student develops a plan of action.

You will notice that the student self-assessment form guides students to focus on only one or two specific aspects, or traits, of the work. These desired traits should be clearly articulated to students. In fact, students and teachers alike may use checklists (for cross-checking work against the required criteria) and rubrics (guides to scoring) as part of the assessment and evaluation process. These methods are transparent, providing the expected qualities and values of student work.

THE ROLE OF ASSESSMENT IN THE INSTRUCTIONAL CYCLE

A critical aspect of developing and maintaining the delivery of quality education is monitoring what is learned from assessments and using this information to inform instructional decisions. In other words, exemplary teachers use information from student performance on assessments to plan and shape instruction in an ongoing manner.

Leahy, Lyon, Thompson, and Wiliam (2005, p. 19) assert that traditional approaches to assessment reflect a "quality control" approach, where the instruc-

My Strengths and Areas to Improve

Trait(s):

Name:

Name of paper:

Date:

My Opinion

My strengths are:

What I think I need to work on is:

My Teacher's or Classmate's Opinion

Strengths include:

Work on:

My Plan

What I will do now is:

Next time I'll ask for feedback from:

FIGURE 6.6. Student self-assessment form. From Stiggins, Arter, Chappuis, and Chappuis (2004). Adapted by permission from the authors and the Association for Supervision and Curriculum Development.

tion and assessment process involves teaching the curriculum and then determining who did and didn't meet the objectives, much like a "quality control approach in manufacturing." They suggest a shift toward a "quality assurance" approach, where teaching is adapted, if necessary, as learning occurs. When such an approach is embraced, the focus transfers from teaching to learning and the line separating instruction and assessment becomes indistinct due to the potential for all activities to provide a better picture of student understanding.

As discussed in Chapter 3, the instructional cycle we describe has four phases:

➢ Planning for literacy–technology integration

➢ Implementing meaningful, purpose-driven instruction

➢ Assessing student learning

➢ Assessing and reflecting on instruction

Here we focus on the role of assessment within each of these phases. While in the first phase, planning for literacy–technology integration, teachers develop assessment plans for instruction; they may use information gathered from previous assessments to assist them in determining these instructional plans. Data collected from diagnostic, formative, and/or summative assessments are also useful while implementing meaningful, purpose-driven instruction, with assessment guiding instruction as it unfolds. During the third phase, assessing student learning, assessment is implemented to assist teachers in tailoring plans and instruction best to meet student needs. While the fourth phase, assessing and reflecting on instruction, is underway, teachers allocate additional time to reflect on their instruction based in part on the assessment data they analyze. The instructional cycle is ongoing, with assessment continuously informing each phase in the cycle.

Let's consider Harmony's work with fifth graders as they engage in Book Club, a framework that includes reading, writing, and both whole-class and small-group discussion (Raphael, Pardo, Highfield, & McMahon, 1997).

Planning Informed by Assessment

Harmony thoughtfully develops a lesson progression designed to parallel students' interests, meet requirements of the fifth-grade curriculum, draw upon existing resources (e.g., literature, software), and satisfy the following state standards (Minnesota Department of Education, 2003):

> ➤ To analyze, interpret, evaluate and appreciate a wide variety of fiction.
> ➤ Use information found in electronic and print media.

She carefully selects high-quality literature featuring dogs that represents a range in reading level, cultural diversity, genre, and sex of protagonist, while honoring her commitment to align books with students' needs and interests. Harmony determines that she will read *Where the Red Fern Grows* (Rawls, 1961) aloud and that students will choose a book such as *Because of Winn-Dixie* (DiCamillo, 2000) or *Shiloh* (Naylor, 1991) to read as part of their small-group discussion. Harmony selects websites for students to review that provide information on hounds and coon hunting, thus enhancing their understanding of the context of *Where the Red Fern Grows*. She is aware that determining an assessment plan while organizing the lesson progression is critical; therefore, she takes steps to develop such a plan.

First, Harmony prepares a note-taking sheet to guide students during their online search. She plans to examine the information they record to determine if they successfully found what she intended. If they did not, Harmony will reteach, providing additional opportunities for practice. Second, she decides that as students engage in the read-aloud of *Where the Red Fern Grows* and the reading of their individually chosen books, she will check for comprehension at regular intervals; student responses will inform Harmony of their ability to connect with the text. Third, students' level of engagement and demonstrated ability to think critically, examined in part through observation during the whole-class and individual work on character development, will lead Harmony to take specific actions designed to meet individual needs. Fourth, Harmony will follow students' ability to reflect in their journals on how the dogs in their Book Club selections played a role in a character's development over time and compare this relationship to that between Billie and his dogs in *Where the Red Fern Grows*; these written responses will determine student capability to analyze, contrast, and compare texts. Across all of the assessments, Harmony will consider student effectiveness with traditional print literacy, electronic literacy, and the use of technology to accomplish literacy-related goals.

Instruction Guided by Assessment

With the planning phase complete, the first lesson opens with students engaged in an online search, using the provided note-taking sheet. Harmony reviews students' findings to confirm that they satisfy the learning goals. Then she reads aloud from the focal book, and students select books for Book Club. As the read-aloud continues, Harmony models and engages in a think-aloud about the development of the main character in *Where the Red Fern Grows*. A critical support to this aspect of the lesson is the creation of character maps, updated by students as the story unfolds. Harmony highlights author Rawls's use of descriptive language and the roles of theme and setting in the development of the story. As planned, she regularly checks for comprehension. She also follows student understanding of character development by carefully listening to students' discussions, thoughtfully reviewing their recorded reflections in their journals, and deliberately monitoring their creation of character maps using software. It goes without saying that Harmony observes her students in an ongoing manner as they engage in the opportunities embedded within this learning experience.

Assessment Informing Planning and Instruction

Upon completion of the lessons related to Book Club, Harmony and each student review the character map completed using software. She records reflective comments, and so does the student. Together they determine if they will include the item in the student's portfolio. On a more personal note, Harmony reflects on her role as a facilitator of learning. She recognizes the significance of careful planning, intentional instruction, and the role of assessment throughout each lesson. It becomes increasingly obvious to her that over the course of the unit she has learned much about students' levels of understanding, and she uses this knowledge to plan future learning opportunities.

Throughout the lesson progression, Harmony was cognizant of the need to align instruction with assessment. Like Harmony, you can engage in this cycle. As you do, it is useful to consider the degree to which your assessments are: aligned with your instruction, authentic, unbiased, meaningful, engaging, and within a student's zone of proximal development (Norton & Wiberg, 1998).

NEW POSSIBILITIES WITH TECHNOLOGY

Technology can assist in literacy assessment and in the assessment of technology skills themselves. At the very least, technology provides a storage site for artifacts related to student interests, observational notes taken during the delivery of instruction, and information gained from students during process interviews. Another role of technology in the area of literacy is monitoring how students progress from one stage of competence to another. For example, in reading, the teacher and students can access leveled readers online, providing an electronic record of what has been read. Students can also participate in an online conversation with others reading the same book; all involved can share their reactions to the reading and make predictions about events. This record of online sharing can be another form of assessment for teachers. In the area of writing, students can word-process drafts and teachers and peers can provide feedback directly in the document, with students revising and editing alongside the feedback. Interested parties may follow drafts as they unfold and gain insights into writing processes.

In addition to using technology in the development of portfolio entries, such as a word-processed report, entire portfolios may now be developed using hypermedia and other carefully designed software programs. Programs such as these assist in the storage and organization of portfolio entries. As described by Clarke and Agne (1997) in Norton and Wiburg (2003), advantages of such a system include: providing an opportunity to follow student growth along various routes within one piece, offering learners a convenient method for editing their portfolios by easily adding and connecting new artifacts, and encouraging browsing without sifting through a large volume of papers.

Many states are in the process of developing and implementing online assessments to be used by students. For example, Jinna's and Jon David's students engage in districtwide electronic assessment, which yields rapid feedback on their performance.

REFLECTIVE PRACTICE

Sykes (1999) points out the significance of critical and reflective inquiry along with the importance of linking teacher learning to student learning. The definition of *reflection* that suits our work is the practice or art of analyzing actions, decisions, or products by focusing on the process of achieving them (Killion & Todnem, 1991). Teacher reflection on learning enhances understanding of what expected outcomes students are accomplishing and to what degree they are being accomplished. Reflection may also provide a snapshot of the effectiveness of instruction, yielding suggestions for ways to improve the presentation of content. Leia suggests:

" . . . when I've been developing these different ways to integrate technology into my classroom, I have this picture in my head of how it's going to turn out. Kind of what my expectations and objectives are. I think being able to do the work of analyzing and answering the question 'Did they meet the objectives?' helps me to step back and reflect on how I'm going to do this differently next time. How can I bridge to the next thing? What went wrong? What went really well?"

Reflective questions such as these can promote effective decision making, leading to improved delivery of instruction and enhanced student learning.

In the next chapter, we consider the importance of teachers assuming the role of change agent.

INQUIRY AND REFLECTION

An effective way to monitor student progress and gain valuable insights to inform planning and instruction is to examine student work closely. Select two students whose literacy progress concerns you and for each choose two pieces of work involving new literacies. Meet with a colleague to discuss these work samples. Use these prompts to guide your discussion and extend your thinking:

 ➢ What is my initial interpretation of this work?

 ➢ What did the student accomplish in producing this work?

 ➢ What has the student said about this work that can help me better understand his or her work process as well as the product?

 ➢ How can I best support the student in moving to the next level of understanding, taking into account his or her strengths and instructional needs?

Record in your anecdotal log insights gained from this activity. More specifically, consider what you learned about the students and their progress as well as your planning, instruction, and assessment. Perhaps most important, examine how this experience will shape the literacy–technology learning opportunities you provide your students in the future.

CHAPTER 7

THE TEACHER AS CHANGE AGENT IN THE LITERACY–TECHNOLOGY LEARNING ENVIRONMENT

Our computer lab is still very temperamental, so there's been a certain amount of stress in deciding whether it's worth the kids getting frustrated if the computer crashes or the printer won't print. But it's been so fun and exciting to see how you can reach kids that you don't reach in other ways and I think, especially for kids who don't have technology at home, that this is their only chance to really use the computer.

So what an opportunity we have given them.

—JINNA, classroom teacher

Well, I think I didn't know I would be a computer guru at the school, that people kind of look at me a little more that way.

—JON DAVID, classroom teacher

We first met Jinna and Jon David when they were preservice teachers enrolled in Carolyn's block of literacy methods courses. We had just begun our journey to integrate technology into our methods courses, and Jinna and Jon David were part of the cadre of students who experienced our early efforts. We modeled technology-embedded reading and writing instruction and assigned projects requiring the use of technology for instructional planning and professional development. As you might guess, Jinna and Jon David did well on their assignments, and their passion for working with children was evident in their school-based field placements. We decided to follow Jinna, Jon David, and a handful of others in their first year of teaching. We were curious to know about the challenges they faced and the rewards they reaped with literacy–technology integration in their new classrooms.

At the beginning of the first year of Jon David's teaching career, he put into practice several techniques we had modeled in our methods courses, using software and websites we had introduced. By the middle of that year, he was experimenting with new techniques, and we found ourselves learning from him about new software and websites to enhance students' learning and teacher professional development. As a first-year teacher, Jon David asked if he could attend a few meetings of the established technology committee in his building. By the end of the year, he was working with the committee on the acquisition of specific software and hardware to enable a project he wanted to do with his second graders. We thought of Jon David then as we do today with respect to technology integration: as an advocate for his students and a leader in his building. Recently, we asked Jon David how he sees himself with respect to literacy–technology integration. He chose his words carefully: adventurous, flexible, and a learner.

Jinna began her teaching career with eight fifth-grade students in a school largely serving homeless families. Like Jon David, she began that first year with hopes of implementing methods and materials introduced to her during her teacher preparation, but whereas Jon David entered a school setting with a computer lab and building technology specialist in place, Jinna's school had only a small space for a lab that had not yet been set up. For the first half of that first year, Jinna's only access to technology was her personal computer. Certainly, Jinna could have changed her mind about the importance of integrating technology into her instruction. Instead, she changed her mind about *how* she would integrate it, focusing her literacy–technology integration on finding resources to inform her practice through lesson plans, professional development articles, and using the Internet to learn about local places she could visit with her students. Furthermore, she continued to brainstorm ideas and note resources to tap when the technology lab did become operational, and it did. In fits and starts, the hardware, software, and Internet access became functional, and as they did Jinna was prepared to engage her students in new literacies. Despite many setbacks and frustrations, Jinna persisted and maintained her belief that her students could and would engage in practices of higher-order thinking and new literacies enabled by computers and the Internet.

UNDERSTANDING WHAT IT MEANS TO BE A CHANGE AGENT

In 1999, Becker and colleagues found that the vast majority of teachers who integrated technology into their instruction used it to support their current teaching beliefs and practices. In other words, an innovation does not in and of itself lead to innovative practice. Ultimately, it is teachers who shape the ways in which curriculum, instruction, and assessment work, both individually and collectively, best to meet the needs of students. As stated, the teacher's role changes with the integration of technology, becoming more important, not less, in new literacies classrooms (Leu, Kinzer, Coiro, & Cammack, 2004). In fact, we believe that the great potential and possibilities for student learning afforded by new technologies can best be realized when teachers act as change agents.

What does it mean to be an agent of change? It means to be proactive in determining how the change affects students and strategic in managing change. It is not related to how many years you've been teaching, where you teach, or who you teach. While the availability of up-to-date resources is important, teachers with very few resources at their disposal act as change agents every day, often providing leadership in obtaining more resources. In the final analysis, being a change agent is about who you are as a teacher, what you believe about teaching, and what you do on a daily basis in your classroom and for your professional development.

Recent publications document teacher work that is truly innovative, involving new technologies, new approaches to teaching, and changing teacher beliefs. In this chapter, we draw from our own research on teacher practices as well as the growing body of literature in this area to investigate the ways in which teachers are acting as change agents and, in so doing, becoming the conduit through which new technologies enhance and increase student learning. We address the topic of change from the perspective of how teachers can contribute to the course of change rather than merely carrying out change efforts conceived by others who are often outside of the everyday classroom experience.

We begin with a focus on the attributes, attitudes, and actions of teachers who act as change agents as they integrate literacy and new technologies. We then discuss the ways in which attributes, attitudes, and actions are related to one another. In the next section, we address the topic of personal professional development, including reflection. We then take a broad view of the changing landscape of teaching. Finally, we return to the overarching concept of change as we examine technology integration as a dimension of change.

CHARACTERISTICS ASSOCIATED WITH TEACHER AGENCY

Based on what we've observed in our work and the work of others, we find it helpful to classify characteristics associated with change agents along three dimensions related to teaching: attributes, attitudes, and actions. In this section we describe each of these in detail.

Teacher Attributes

Teachers who act as change agents possess certain attributes. They are decision makers, they are confident, and they possess vision.

Change Agents Are Decision Makers

Although effective teachers embrace the idea that new technologies offer new possibilities, both for teaching and for student learning, we find that those who most effectively integrate technology into their teaching practices are also the most critical consumers. Teachers who effectively integrate technology into their literacy instruction do not believe that just because it is new technology, it automatically fits with good practice. Just because it can be done doesn't mean it should be.

Decision makers are not afraid to let go of a plan or an instructional approach that is not working. They come to their lessons prepared with a plan B and a plan C, and they are not afraid to go to these backup plans when necessary. One of the benefits of achieving a comfort level with this sort of flexibility is that your students learn from your example how to respond when things do not go as planned. They also learn that when a plan falls out of alignment with the goal that it is designed to reach, it is more important to serve the goal than to stick with the plan. Confidence is important for students to have in order to function healthily and successfully in a world propelled by change.

Teachers who are effective instructional decision makers are keenly aware of the downside of trying too much too soon, often opting to integrate less technology to ensure that it is done well. Darin's practice exemplifies this quality. As a second-year teacher, he became the de facto technology specialist in an alternative school simply because he had more expertise with technology than any of the other teachers and there was no building technology specialist. He found this role so fulfilling that, by the end of that school year, he stated that he could see himself as a technology specialist one day. The next year, he took a position in another state and did very little with technology integration, choosing instead to immerse himself in the state learning standards, all of which were new to him. At the end of that year, he described himself in relation to technology integration as simultaneously eager and hesitant. As he put it, "I'm anxious to learn of new technology integration ideas; however, I'm hesitant to implement them if I don't feel that they'll be meaningful to the students."

Effective teachers have a solid understanding of the content and methods associated with a strong print-based curriculum, and they do not take on more than they can manage while maintaining best practices. They are thoughtful in their decision making during all phases of the instructional process—as they gather information to inform instruction, as they plan for instruction, as they implement instruction, as they assess student learning, and as they reflect on their own practice.

Change Agents Are Confident

Confidence, or self-efficacy, is an important factor to consider in any change process. Change agents possess self-efficacy, meaning that they believe in their ability to learn to design and present meaningful technology-embedded instruction. This does not mean that their early attempts are always successful or that they enjoy consistent success once their journey is well underway. It means that they believe success is *possible*, and it is this belief in possibilities that turns confidence into action, leading them to take the steps necessary to achieve their goals.

Teachers at different points in their careers may experience different levels of confidence in the face of new technologies. For teachers at the beginning of their careers, experiencing self-efficacy with technology integration may be a challenge because their sense of self-efficacy related to teaching in general is still developing. Teachers early in their careers have informed us that it can be difficult to think about integrating technology into literacy instruction because they have so many other demands to juggle and everything is new. They have also observed that there may be few or no teachers in the building equipped to mentor a new teacher with respect to literacy–technology integration because they have not been doing it themselves. On the other hand, beginning teachers have the benefit of viewing new technologies as an integral part of literacy learning from the start.

For experienced teachers, expertise that has been cultivated over many years may actually hinder the implementation of new technologies. Research on the influx of computers and technology into schools indicates that there is a wide range of reactions, with many teachers reluctant to make a change from what is familiar (McGrail, 2004). Change may feel less comfortable and also less necessary for effective teaching. The further away teachers are from their preservice preparation, the less likely it is that they were exposed to technology as a part of that preparation. Thus, their concept of literacy may not include technology, and they may have limited models of literacy–technology integration to draw upon.

Change Agents Have Vision

We suspect that most teachers who have been highly successful in their literacy–technology integration, some affecting thousands of children with their work, began with a simple vision: to design one meaningful and engaging learning experience for their students. This is certainly what Mark Ahlness (2005) had in mind when he developed an environmental education project for his third graders in the early 1990s. That project, like so many others with similar beginnings, went on to win the Miss Rumphius Award, which honors educators who share exceptional literacy–technology teaching ideas online (*www.reading.org/resources/community/links_rumphius_links.html*).

Ahlness's idea was to borrow paper grocery bags from a local market, have his students decorate them with environmental artwork and slogans in honor of Earth Day, and return them to the market for bagging customers' groceries on Earth Day. In Mark's own words, "Sometimes a little idea grows into a movement" (p. 28). Though he was unsure of the technical details, Mark's excitement about the possibilities of the Internet led to his taking the Earth Day Groceries Project (*www.earthdaybags.org*) online in 1994, where it remains, affecting teachers, children, and grocery shoppers in communities around the world.

What is intriguing about vision as a characteristic of teachers who effectively infuse technology into their instruction is that it is constantly evolving. Many teachers do not begin with a clear-cut vision of what they want to do or how they want to do it. In other words, they are often unsure of exactly what their vision is until they get more information and begin to experiment. For these teachers, the vision is shaped and refined by the journey. What is important is that they have a sense of possibility that motivates them to see beyond their current ways of doing things. The future may be unclear, but it is on the horizon, and it is expansive.

Teacher Attitudes

A positive attitude adds much to a teacher's potential to be a change agent. We find that teacher beliefs in three areas are particularly important: beliefs about the value of technology integration, beliefs about the abilities of their students, and beliefs about their role as teachers.

Change Agents Believe That New Technologies Can Enhance Literacy Instruction

In our work with teachers, we consistently ask them to share their views on meaningful technology integration. Laura's words echo our sentiments: "You do not do technology just to do it. You think about what you want to teach and then how does technology make it better."

Teachers who are agents of change do not integrate technology into instruction solely because their administrators tell them they must, because they find it convenient to do so, or because their students lobby for it. Ultimately, teachers who act as change agents come to a belief that there is merit in becoming technologically literate. Furthermore, they believe that the new literacies of the Internet and other information and communication technologies (ICTs) consist of a broadening range of skills and strategies including and expanding upon traditional print-based literacies. While they see the domain of literate activity becoming broader, they believe that new literacies and print-based literacies can coexist in the classroom, the presence of each supporting the other.

Change Agents Believe That All Students Can Engage in the New Literacies

As we have stated repeatedly, what it takes to be considered literate in the 21st century requires higher-level thinking and the coordination of many more skills and strategies than have previously been associated with literacy. Teachers who act as change agents integrate technology in ways that work against current inequities in reading and writing achievement, creating new classroom dynamics and opening the door to higher-level learning opportunities for an increasing number of students. Teachers who effectively integrate technology into their instruction believe that their students—including their "low readers," their English language learners, and their special education students—can interact with technology in meaningful ways. These teachers integrate technology into the fabric of their teaching of all students, not just some.

Change Agents Believe That Their Role Is to Be Proactive

A final note regarding teacher attitudes: change agents believe that the new literacies are worth teaching, that all students can participate in learning them, and, most important, that it is their responsibility to lead students to attain them.

Teacher Actions

Teachers who act as change agents share the distinction of behaving in certain ways with both their students and their colleagues. Specifically, they communicate and collaborate with others, they explore new territory, and they are persistent in the face of barriers.

Change Agents Communicate and Collaborate with Others

Teachers who are actively seeking to improve their instruction with technology share their ideas with one another (Labbo, 2005a). They transcend traditional views of teaching as an isolated profession and engage themselves in a community of teacher-learners. They make this happen in many ways—by talking with colleagues, initiating e-mail correspondence, and participating in professional discussion groups, to name a few. Face-to-face discussion groups and study groups are increasing in popularity, as are online discussion groups such as RTEACHER, a listserv sponsored by the International Reading Association for discussing issues related to literacy and technology (*www.reading.org/resources/community/discussions_rt_about.html*). Whether by talking or writing, teachers are change agents when they are in communication with others, sharing their expertise and drawing upon that of their colleagues.

Communication and collaboration with colleagues is a central component in ongoing professional development and critically important in the age of new literacies, but change agents also communicate and collaborate with their students. Communication with students involves getting to know them and their interests and experiences, especially with regard to reading, writing, and technology. Teachers benefit from careful observation of and one-on-one communication with students. Furthermore, they propel their students to higher levels of learning as they engage in and engender discussion and *tentative talk* (Allington & Johnston, 2002, p. 214).

In classrooms where tentative talk is encouraged, conversation is an important tool for learning. Participation in learning conversations is not limited to students who can provide the correct answer. The idea behind tentative talk is that talk is not only a way to demonstrate knowledge that has already been acquired, but can also serve as a mechanism for the acquisition of knowledge. Partially correct answers are encouraged, and students are urged to use their peers' comments as a foundation for further talk.

In addition to communicating with others, change agents work alongside both other teachers and students to meet goals. Sometimes this means that a group of teachers teaching similar content will collaboratively plan and/or deliver instruction. Other times, it means that teachers will share ideas and cull what they need to pursue their individual teaching goals. Other times, collaboration is a natural outgrowth of communication as teachers use each other's ideas as launchpads for further discovery.

Change Agents Explore New Territory

By now, it should be obvious that change agents do not rely solely on what has come before. A large part of what they do is actively explore new territory and seek out new possibilities. When we first read the collection of firsthand accounts of literacy–technology integration by teachers awarded the Miss Rumphius Award (Karchmer, Mallette, Kara-Soteriou, & Leu, 2005), we were struck by the number of teachers who referred to their experiences as a journey. We have used this term to describe our own experiences as teacher educators, and we have heard many of our colleagues in the arenas of teacher education and research use the same term. It captures the essence of traveling a path that has not yet been marked as well as the aura of discovery related to new technologies.

Traveling such a path requires a willingness not to know for sure and to make that "not knowing" public. Teachers try new software with students only to abandon it midstream because a quick cost–benefit analysis reveals that it isn't promoting the learning that was planned. Teachers wait to implement lessons until they can do so with the support of a knowledgeable other such as a technology specialist or teacher colleague. The teacher is caught in the act of not knowing and, therefore, learning. Coiro (2005a) puts it simply when she advises, "Take a few risks along the way" (p. 212).

Change Agents Persist When Faced with Barriers

At the start of this chapter, we described two very different first-year teaching experiences with technology. The barriers faced by Jinna were transparent and pervasive, yet Jon David faced his own set of barriers. While his teaching setting was resource-rich compared to many, his vision and goals exceeded the available resources. For Jon David, persistence meant persuading the technology committee to put funds toward the acquisition of new hardware and software, talking to technology resource staff outside of his building, and making connections online to continue his learning.

All teachers who integrate technology into their instruction face barriers routinely. Technology fails. URLs become inactive. The server goes down. The school's firewall keeps students from getting to a website that they are supposed to be able to access. No one else in the building is doing what you want to do. Everyone else in the building is way ahead of what you want to do! All teachers face barriers routinely, whether they are using technology or not, but good teachers know how to swim with the tide rather than going against it and see learning opportunities even in the face of barriers.

The Relationship among Attributes, Attitudes, and Actions

It is important to recognize that attributes, attitudes, and actions are interdependent and subject to change. They do not exist in a vacuum, and they are not static. For example, current attributes and attitudes may lead to certain actions, but actions can also lead to a change in attributes and attitudes. For example, it can take confidence to initiate communication with a teacher you do not know in hopes of learning more about technology integration, but your confidence will undoubtedly increase once you have learned what your new colleague has to share with you. It can also take confidence to share information with others who may see you as a role model or mentor when you have never looked at yourself in this way before. Yet assuming that role by sharing with others may affect your own confidence level. Even a task as simple as going to a new website can feel daunting at first, but spending time at a new site leads to increased knowledge, which affects vision, confidence, and decision making. Teachers' actions reflect their current attributes and attitudes—that is, who they are and what they believe—but also shape who they are and who they will become.

THE IMPORTANCE OF PERSONAL PROFESSIONAL DEVELOPMENT

What has perhaps struck us the most is the degree to which change agents take their professional development personally, taking responsibility for it and actively seeking it out. Coiro (2005a) reports that teachers who effectively integrate literacy and technology take a proactive approach to learning in which they seek authentic professional development experiences.

Ongoing professional development is necessary for anyone seeking to maintain high-quality instructional practice. Needless to say, the rapidly changing nature of technology makes ongoing professional development even more important. We have noticed that those who effectively integrate new technologies into their instruction have a very personal approach to professional development, not only taking advantage of workshops and other opportunities offered or required by their school districts, but also actively seeking out opportunities for professional development. For these teachers, professional development is ongoing, occurs in multiple contexts, and revolves around communication with colleagues, locally and globally, in person and online.

Labbo (2005a) describes the importance of "making the cutting edge a comfortable place to be" (p. 167), and notes the wide array of opportunities for personal professional development that are now available online, including staff development tutorials, journal articles, mentoring, listservs, bulletin boards, and discussion forums. *Reading Online* (*www.readingonline.org*), published by the International Reading Association, for example, is an electronic journal with links embedded in its articles. As mentioned earlier in this book, teachers can access lesson plans, exchange ideas, and reflect on their practice by visiting the ReadWriteThink website (*www.readwritethink.org*), and the National Council of Teachers of English offers a year-long module for teachers interested in an inquiry approach to learning through reading and writing (*www.ncate.org/profdev*).

For teachers who are the first in their building or district to infuse technology into the curriculum, informal online communities can provide a needed backbone of professional support. E-mail allows teachers to sit down when it fits their schedule and be part of a larger community. When Darin was teaching at an alternative school and was dubbed the technology expert in the building, he said that he often "felt like an island, in terms of technology." His e-mail correspondence with teachers in similar settings helped get him through that year and support him as he supported others in the building with technology integration.

Finally, effective teachers are those who seek more than the acquisition of new technology skills from professional development opportunities. They seek information, conversation, and thought about what those skills mean for reading and writing development. In a chapter called "How I Became an Exemplary Teacher (Although I'm Really Still Learning Just Like Anyone Else)," Day (2001) states that one of the common features associated with exemplary first-grade teachers is that they find staff development experiences that focus on *understanding the reasons behind methods* rather than just learning methods or strategies. With this level of knowledge, they are equipped to be effective decision makers as they explore numerous possibilities for literacy–technology integration.

THE IMPORTANCE OF REFLECTION

The body of research on teacher effectiveness supports the notion that teachers should be reflective decision makers, not mere technicians. High-quality teaching requires more than the demonstration of basic competencies; teachers benefit from regularly evaluating and analyzing their teaching behaviors as well as the thoughts and understandings that drive these behaviors. Zeichner and Liston (1996, p. 6) characterize a reflective teacher as one who:

> ➢ examines, frames, and attempts to solve the dilemmas of classroom practice;
>
> ➢ is aware of and questions the assumptions and values he or she brings to teaching;
>
> ➢ is attentive to the institutional and cultural contexts in which he or she teaches;
>
> ➢ takes part in curriculum development and is involved in school change efforts; and
>
> ➢ takes responsibility for his or her own professional development.

Change, in this case the integration of new technologies into teaching, can be a strong catalyst for teacher reflection. The process of figuring out how best to incorporate new technologies into the classroom and new literacies into the curriculum begs for an examination of current practices, including the beliefs and values that support them.

Communication and collaboration can also be a tremendous support for reflective teaching. The teachers we work with report that coming together in a safe and trusted community is a central component in their reflective practice. They find that talking about their practice and hearing about other approaches leads to a critical examination that they would not engage in on their own. It is enlightening to them to hear other perspectives on the teaching dilemmas they describe. They also benefit from putting into words their accounts of where they are in their teaching and their journey of literacy–technology integration. Finally, engaging in self-assessment through writing spurs teacher reflection. Teachers have learned a great deal through their regular entries in anecdotal logs and instructional planning grids, as described in Chapter 3.

THE CHANGING ROLE OF TEACHERS AND THE CHANGING LANDSCAPE OF TEACHING

It is clear from the National Educational Technology Standards for Teachers (NETS•T) that the role of the teacher and related teacher competencies are different than they were even 10 years ago. The International Society for Technology in Education has established six teacher competency areas related to technology integration (see Figure 7.1).

Just as the Internet and other ICTs offer broad learning associated with new literacies, these new technologies offer teachers new ways to interact with each other and to improve their practice. Through "on-demand, anytime, anyplace access to professional development resources online" (Labbo, 2005b, p. 343), teachers are able to access recent research findings and new teaching ideas quickly and conveniently. Using online teacher communities, online publications, and classroom websites, teachers can empower themselves on their journeys of literacy–technology integration.

Furthermore, there has been a steady increase in the number of Internet resources for teaching and learning that are teacher developed. The traditional model of teacher development as a top-down process, with teachers passively receiving information and ideas to inform their practice, is no longer sufficient. Teachers are joining in the process of creating and disseminating good ideas and information about the new literacies. They are actively involved in creating the new knowledge that is directing the field.

Our knowledge of the content and processes related to literacy–technology integration is still in the formative stages and, as noted in Chapter 1, rapidly

- Technology Operations and Concepts
  ○ Teachers demonstrate a sound understanding of technology operations and concepts.
- Planning and Designing Learning Environments and Experiences
  ○ Teachers plan and design effective learning environments and experiences supported by technology.
- Teaching, Learning, and the Curriculum
  ○ Teachers implement curriculum plans that include methods and strategies for applying technology to maximize students' learning.
- Assessment and Evaluation
  ○ Teachers apply technology to facilitate a variety of effective assessment and evaluation strategies.
- Productivity and Professional Practice
  ○ Teachers use technology to enhance their productivity and professional practice.
- Social, Ethical, Legal, and Human Issues
  ○ Teachers understand the social, ethical, legal, and human issues surrounding the use of technology in PreK–12 schools and apply those principles in practice.

FIGURE 7.1. Competencies expected of teachers leaving preservice teacher education programs. Reprinted with permission from the National Educational Technology Standards for Teachers: Connecting Curriculum and Technology, copyright ©2000, ISTE® (International Society for Technology in Education), *iste@iste.org*, *www.iste.org*. All rights reserved. Permission does not constitute an endorsement by ISTE.

changing. As a classroom teacher experimenting with various aspects of literacy–technology integration, you will add to this knowledge base, especially as you share what you learn with others. All in all, as a field, we have great potential to move away from isolation and toward community.

UNDERSTANDING TECHNOLOGY INTEGRATION AS A DIMENSION OF CHANGE

> We have become so accustomed to the presence of change that we rarely stop to think what change really means as we are experiencing it at the personal level. . . . The crux of change is how individuals come to grips with this reality.
>
> —MICHAEL FULLEN, educational researcher

Change is inevitable. Anyone who has been teaching for more than a couple of years at the elementary, middle, secondary, or college level can attest to this fact. But the development of the computer, the Internet, and other ICTs that make up the new technologies may well be the biggest change that educators will see in this lifetime. Over the course of the past 10 to 15 years, teachers across the United States have witnessed this change. The single computer that once sat in a corner of the library media center turned into a bank of computers along the wall, which then became a computer cluster in the middle of the room. Soon, there was an entire computer lab and, after that, individual computers in classrooms that slowly evolved into classroom computer clusters or sets of laptops with Internet access.

The new technologies of the Internet and other ICTs have changed the very definition of literacy and, therefore, of what it means to teach literacy. They have changed not only the way in which we work, but the kind of work we do. In large part, this book has been about examining change—in learning environments, lesson planning, instruction, and assessment as well as in professional attributes, attitudes, and actions.

Michael Fullen (2001, p. 39), a widely acclaimed authority on educational reform, states that innovation is multidimensional, involving:

➢ the use of new or revised materials or technologies

➢ the use of new teaching approaches

➢ the alteration of beliefs.

While most approaches to innovation include the first dimension, Fullen asserts that very few include the second or third. Yet, in order to affect student learning positively, change is needed along *all three* dimensions. In his words, " . . . changes in beliefs and understanding are the foundation of achieving lasting reform" (p. 45).

Traditionally, teacher education has been the route for developing teacher understanding, knowledge, and beliefs. For preservice teachers, this has involved literacy methods courses and field placements. For inservice teachers, it has involved district- and buildingwide staff development opportunities, often in the form of workshops, mentoring, and annual teacher professional development plans. You may recall that our interest in and concern for new literacies was prompted by our responsibilities in these areas. In the next chapter, we address ways to create and sustain teachers as change agents as we reflect on the lessons we've learned about literacy–technology integration in our professional lives and through the lives of elementary school teachers.

INQUIRY AND REFLECTION

In this chapter, we discussed personal professional development and reflection as qualities associated with teachers who act as change agents. The teachers with whom we work find the instructional planning grid helpful in motivating them and holding them accountable, not only for instructional planning, but also for reflection after having taught with technology. Use the instructional planning grid in Appendix G to record your instructional goals, instructional preparation, observed evidence of learning, and future instructional plans related to technology integration. Commit to updating it weekly for a period of 1 month or more. In your anecdotal log, reflect on your use of technology throughout the instructional cycle: planning for literacy–technology integration; implementing meaningful, purpose-driven instruction; assessing student learning; and assessing and reflecting on instruction.

CHAPTER 8

THE IMPACT OF TECHNOLOGY ON OUR JOURNEY AS TEACHERS

Looking Back, Looking Forward

> How do we best prepare students for the new literacies that will define their future? Quite possibly that is the single greatest challenge we face in literacy education today.
> —LEU, MALLETTE, KARCHMER, AND KARA-SOTERIOU (2005, p. 1)

As Miss Rumphius Award–winning teacher Gino Sanguiliano (2005) reflects on his journey of integrating literacy and technology, he writes, "I am not sure how much longer we can refer to the knowledge of the Internet, computers, and other technologies as new literacies. In fact, as far as our students are concerned, they are anything but" (p. 25). Sanguiliano goes on to relay a story about his 3-year-old's ability to turn on a computer, get online, go to a bookmarked website, and play a game, all independent of adult help. We have similar stories about our children—stories that would have been fantasy when we were young.

Children are ready for new literacies, and many are already engaged in them. Much of their continued learning will occur in the care of teachers, and they will learn by example. The examples set by teachers need to prepare children for multimedia communication, the ability to coordinate complex comprehension strategies, and critical analysis and evaluation. In addition, children need to leave school prepared to work both independently and collaboratively as they embark on a lifetime of continued learning. In order to meet this considerable challenge, we need new ways of approaching the task of teaching.

In the previous chapters, we considered new perspectives on the classroom environment for promoting student learning as well as the ways in which teachers can structure their own learning and ongoing professional development. In addition, we have taken an in-depth look at the impact of new technologies on the planning, teaching, and assessment phases of the instructional process. Most recently, in Chapter 7, we asserted that even in the midst of unprecedented technological advances, the teacher remains the most critical agent of change. We devote this final chapter to the lessons we've learned thus far on our literacy–technology integration journey, both from our experiences in the college classroom and from the experiences of our colleagues in elementary school classrooms. We also present the surprises we've encountered along the way. Finally, we address what we believe to be the key issues in literacy–technology integration as we look toward the future.

LOOKING BACK: PAVING THE WAY FOR CHANGE

As we reflect on the journey of integrating technology into our own teaching, we are challenged to consider our beginnings and how we have grown as teachers. In the fall of 2000, as we prepared to teach courses we had taught several times before, we felt anxious about meeting the challenge of integrating technology into our instruction. As we embarked on this journey, we often felt that hardware, software, and the Internet were leading us, rather than the other way around. We found ourselves perplexed as we tried to imagine how and why it would be more valuable to have students access course materials online rather than in the classroom and why we needed to introduce them to software such as Inspiration when students could create concept maps with paper and pencil.

Despite our concerns, our tentative first steps bore fruit. As that year unfolded, we were struck by the depth of learning that we observed, not only in our students, but also in ourselves. Our learning curve was steep. Each week, we tried new things with our students. Between class meetings, we studied, explored, practiced, and made choices as we prepared for future literacy–technology integration efforts. We found ourselves modeling the use of new technologies and engaging our students with them in ways that, quite literally, we could not imagine just a few months prior to the school year.

Classroom teachers echo our sentiments when they reflect on their own literacy–technology integration journeys. Our journey took place in the college classroom with adult learners who were on their way to careers in teaching. The journeys of our teacher colleagues took place in the elementary school classroom with children whose career paths were way ahead of them. Nonetheless, our stories are more alike than different. In the next section, we discuss the similarities that cut across our respective teaching communities, using examples from both the elementary school and the college setting. We present these themes as lessons we've learned, and we believe that they represent central aspects of the literacy–technology integration journey.

Lessons Learned along the Way

The seven core components that emerged from our literacy–technology integration journeys, both as teachers of teachers and teachers of children, are: determining what to teach and how to teach it, navigating the tools and the logistics of technology integration, making the most of human resources, engaging in collaboration and communication, engaging in reflection and self-assessment, promoting learning to learn, and making teacher learning transparent to students.

Determining What to Teach and How to Teach It

The first key issue to be resolved in any literacy–technology integration effort is that of figuring out what to teach and how to teach it. This includes consideration of the following questions:

> ➤ How can you design the curriculum so technology supports the tenets of effective literacy instruction?

> ➤ How can you design the curriculum so technology supports your particular students as learners, both in terms of the content to be learned and the process by which they will learn it?

For us, the process of planning what to teach began with looking at our syllabi in their current forms. Though we regularly updated these documents, at their cores they reflected what the literacy education faculty had determined was central to the methods courses. We needed to determine what we were committed to holding on to and how that content might be complemented by the addition of technology. In conjunction with a critical examination of our syllabi, we examined the most recent standards set forth by the National Council for the Accreditation of Teacher Education (NCATE). For elementary school teachers, the standards outlined in the No Child Left Behind Act (2002) must be considered.

We have found that whether you are a well-established teacher or at the very beginning of your career, you will face your own challenges and reap your own benefits during the process of integrating technology into your instruction. For example, one of the benefits and challenges of being an early-career teacher is that your planning canvas is clean; you can begin with technology as an integral part of your plans. For established teachers, the benefit and challenge is having a history of what's worked, which can be a strong foundation upon which to build but also a barrier to new ideas.

Navigating the Tools and the Logistics of Technology Integration

Jon David, Laura, Darin, Leia, Jinna, and Gail all needed to learn about the hardware and software available to them, and they all devoted considerable time to reviewing software and websites designed to support literacy instruction at the elementary school level. This process helped them clarify their goals for literacy–

technology integration and, in some cases, led them to request the purchase of additional software and/or supportive hardware. As they and we began to bring hardware, software, and the Internet into the classroom, we learned that managing the logistics of technology implementation was an important part of the process. Toward this end, we attended faculty development presentations and became familiar with department protocol for reserving equipment for our classrooms as well as computer lab time. Scheduling around the availability of computers became an important consideration as did working with technology support.

Making the Most of Human Resources

We, and many of the classroom teachers described in this book, were extremely fortunate to have available to us not only tools for technology integration, but also (and most important) people who were familiar with these tools and able to help us on our journey. Tapping into the expertise of a building technology specialist has become an integral part of Jon David's and Laura's work as classroom teachers. Whether helping solve a technical problem related to equipment or brainstorming instructional ideas, these individuals provide the support necessary for Jon David and Laura to try new things with their students. When we began our journey, we were assigned a technology fellow, Marcia, who mentored us and enriched our professional development. On leave from her public school teaching position, Marcia assisted us in both planning for and implementing technology integration. Not only did she help us think about ways in which technology might fit into upcoming class sessions, but she also visited one of our classes each week to support the actual instruction.

An important part of our learning to work with those responsible for the technical aspects of technology integration had to do with where to draw the line between our expertise, which focused on literacy instruction, and that of the people who specialized in understanding and quickly addressing technical difficulties when they arose. We learned that integrating technology into our instruction did not mean that we needed to become techies, but we did need to become skilled in seeking the assistance of others and seeing ourselves as part of a team, rather than priding ourselves on the ability to operate with complete autonomy.

Engaging in Collaboration and Communication

As stated several times, ongoing collaboration and communication is a central component of effective literacy–technology integration. For us, it was vital to the achievement of our instructional goals. We regularly discussed with each other and with Marcia how we might effectively plan, implement, and assess learning opportunities with the inclusion of technology. We also communicated with colleagues who taught other courses to the same group of students so that we could facilitate cross-curricular connections as a part of student learning. Aaron, who taught a required educational technology course, was a key resource, as we wanted our work with students to fit cohesively with his. Brad, a universitywide instructional technology consultant, encouraged us to think critically about the role of technology in our teaching. He regularly challenged us first to determine our learning objectives and then to consider whether technology could enhance the likelihood of meeting those objectives. He often reminded us that he didn't view himself as "an advocate for technology" but "an advocate for teaching."

Jinna, Laura, Gail, Darin, Leia, and Jon David have described the positive effect of their participation in a teacher focus group on their ability to integrate technology into their instruction. Darin and Jon David also cite online professional networks as an important source for ideas and support. Furthermore, we have all benefited from visits to our classroom by other teachers, which give us a unique opportunity to debrief our instruction and see it through the eyes of an observer. Our students' work provided us with another perspective. By noting trends in their work that involved or related to technology integration, we saw what they were gleaning from our instruction.

By communicating and collaborating with others, we have been challenged to think in new ways, problem solve, and become more confident in our ability to be successful with technology integration. This confidence has led us to assume increased responsibility for independently offering literacy–technology integration opportunities to our students.

Engaging in Reflection and Self-Assessment

An equally important component of our work was reflection throughout the instructional cycle—as we planned for literacy–technology integration; implemented meaningful, purpose-driven instruction; assessed student learning; and, of course, assessed and reflected on our instruction. As part of our ongoing dialogue with one another, we addressed evidence of student learning based on their contributions to discussion, engagement with technology, and plans for the application of technology integration to their future teaching situations. This reflective process assisted us in monitoring and adjusting our instruction and evaluating the alignment of our short- and long-term goals.

Promoting Learning to Learn

The capacity to adapt to change and learn throughout the lifespan has never been felt as acutely as it is now, in the early 21st century. Our journeys have taught us that students in the elementary grades as well as adult learners benefit from experiences that allow them to learn how to learn. Jon David experienced this truth as he engaged his second graders in various inquiry projects, as did Laura, Gail, Leia, and Darin in different contexts. Furthermore, these teachers witnessed their students' capacities to learn about new technologies through sophisticated questioning and exploration.

In the college classroom, we found that the experiences that were most meaningful to preservice teachers were those in which they used technology themselves and considered software and websites from the perspectives of both teacher and child to ascertain the purposes and potential benefits and challenges of various applications. Engaging preservice teachers in activities that promoted learning to learn proved valuable.

Making Teacher Learning Transparent to Students

None of the teachers we've referenced in this book, ourselves included, waited until they felt expert with new technologies to try them out with students. While we all worked hard to be as prepared as possible, we also knew that trying something new is always a risk and that the most powerful learning often comes through the experience itself. Our classroom environments, at both the elementary and the college level, were safe places to try new things. When our plans took unexpected turns, we didn't shy away from them. Instead, we turned the unexpected into an authentic learning opportunity for our students. We confronted difficulties in front of and often in collaboration with them. By going public with our problems, we shifted the process of solving them into a collective experience—a problem-solving model for our students.

We learned the value of sharing with our students the triumphs and challenges we experienced as we planned for and implemented technology in our own teaching. For example, at the moment of an in-class technical difficulty, we engaged them in a think-aloud about our options: continuing our attempt to solve the problem, calling for technical assistance and engaging students in another experience while waiting to see whether our original plan would be feasible, or deciding to let go of our original plan and implement our backup plan for the day. This transparency provided an opportunity for future teachers to hear and see firsthand the decision-making process we engaged in. While we thought at the time that going public with the challenges we encountered with technology might have some benefit, we now see just how powerful it was. In retrospect, we believe that one of the most important ways in which we taught learning to learn was by making our own learning and reflection transparent.

Surprises Encountered along the Way

In addition to the important lessons we learned as we ventured into the then unknown to us world of new technologies, we had a few very pleasant surprises: becoming self-motivated, becoming confident, and experiencing a true sense of community.

Becoming Self-Motivated

Teachers like Jon David and Laura found that the challenge to integrate technology into the curriculum coupled with their participation in teacher focus groups encouraged them to pursue ways to engage their students in new literacies. Both these teachers and others have said that meeting with others to share what has been learned or done with students provides motivation as well as a healthy sense of accountability. For Laura, regular communication with colleagues challenged her to consider the ways in which she could integrate technology into the curriculum despite the fact she was a first-year teacher. Her perspective was echoed by Leia, who said that participation in a group moved technology integration from the back burner to the front burner.

Along our journey, we found that the more we learned about both the potential of and the challenges inherent in new technologies and the more we observed students of all ages interacting with new technologies, the more excited we became about pursuing very thoughtful literacy–technology integration efforts. Instead of being motivated by an outside source, we became increasingly self-motivated. Similarly, our sense of accountability shifted away from a focus on what we were being told we should do toward what we now understood we needed to do in order to promote students' literacy learning.

Becoming Confident

What is the biggest surprise that most of us encountered along our journey? Laura's simple statement says it all: "I can do it!" Hardly a day goes by that we don't marvel at how far we've come from where we started, and we have heard so many classroom teachers say the same thing, even those whose technology integration efforts have been recognized by others as outstanding. Classroom teacher Gino Sanguiliano describes the beginning of our journey as well as his own when he says, "When I made the decision to truly integrate technology into my curriculum, I did not know how to do it or where to begin" (2005, p. 20). Despite the fact that he is now highly competent in his literacy–technology integration, he describes his initial foray into this new territory as "a huge gamble, to say the least" (p. 20). It is no wonder that we continue to be surprised at our current level of confidence when it comes to literacy–technology integration. For us and for so many other teachers at all levels, this confidence is not about mastering a particular piece of software or understanding all of the necessary cable connections to enable certain uses of technology. Rather, we are confident in the process of learning and moving forward within the context of technological change.

Experiencing a True Sense of Community

One of the biggest concerns of those who study the induction of new teachers into the field and teacher professional development across the career is the isolation that so many teachers experience in their work. The demands of teachers' hectic schedules make it difficult for them to commit to active participation in a learning community, but overcoming these obstacles yields many rewards. Personally, we were surprised by the sense of community that grew out of working with others.

We found that our teaching shifted from being an independent, sometimes isolated endeavor to being part of a larger whole. According to the teachers we've worked with, the relationships cultivated in community inspired and motivated some of their most meaningful work with children. Perhaps Darin's words sum it up best when he says, " . . . we're all sort of struggling in this fight together to make technology meaningful."

LOOKING FORWARD: DEVELOPING AND SUSTAINING TEACHERS FOR THE 21ST CENTURY

> . . . change will always fail until we find some way of developing infrastructures and processes that engage teachers in developing new understandings. . . . we are talking not about surface meaning, but rather deep meaning about new approaches to teaching and learning.
> —FULLEN (2001, pp. 37–38)

The integration of technology into the literacy curriculum presents a new challenge to teachers at all levels, including those responsible for preservice teacher education in the university setting and those responsible for inservice teacher education and professional development in the district setting (Coiro, 2005a; Johnson, 2005; Leu, Kinzer, Coiro, & Cammack, 2004). As of 2006, only 21 states required teachers to demonstrate competence with instructional technology before receiving an initial teaching license (Swanson, 2006). While many teacher preparation programs require preservice teachers to take a course in technology, such coursework does not necessarily translate into the ability to integrate technology effectively into teaching (Milken Exchange on Education Technology and International Society for Technology in Education, 1999). In order for preservice teachers to be prepared for effective literacy–technology integration in their future classrooms, they need to experience such integration in their methods courses (Johnson, 2005; Labbo & Reinking, 1999; Watts Taffe, Gwinn, Johnson, & Horn, 2003). This concept poses a challenge to the status quo, as research indicates that most faculty members do not integrate technology into their instruction (CEO Forum on Education and Technology, 1999). Clearly, a move away from traditional approaches to the teaching of literacy methods courses is needed.

Similarly, developing strategies for effective inservice teacher professional development is a central concern in the age of new literacies. Upon entering the 21st century, school districts in the United States allocated, on average, a mere 6% of their total technology budget to professional development efforts (CEO Forum on Education and Technology, 1999). Providing the hardware, the software, and the Internet access without the infrastructure to support teachers in using them wisely will not result in students acquiring the literacies needed in this century.

Strengthening Support for Teachers

Promoting Leadership in the Classroom

One approach to enhancing teacher effectiveness is the use of instructional coaching. Instructional coaches are master teachers who possess up-to-date, practical knowledge of the classroom environment as well as the ability to put into practice research-based instructional methods. In addition, they possess the ability to build a trusting, nonthreatening relationship with other teachers as they observe teacher practice, listen to teacher concerns, and provide responsive support that moves teachers forward in their instructional understandings and competencies. Our work with Marcia, the mentor assigned to us as part of a technology grant, exemplified the instructional coaching model. Developing a mutual relationship of trust between coach and teacher is the foundational, and often most difficult, dimension of instructional coaching to establish. It cannot occur unless there is a true belief on the part of both the teacher and the instructional coach that the two are working together to support student learning. Instructional coaching is not an approach to teacher evaluation. Rather, it is an approach to professional development with the ultimate goal of enhancing student learning.

One of the benefits of instructional coaching is that it provides teachers with the opportunity to see instruction modeled within the context of their own classrooms. When teachers are actively engaged in the process of observing, analyzing, and reflecting upon demonstration lessons, they can become empowered to generate their own high-caliber lessons. Lyons and Pinnell (2001) and Robb (2000) provide excellent strategies for instructional coaching, including attention to relationship building, classroom observation, and demonstration lessons. In our experience, we have found that demonstration lessons work best when teachers are systematically engaged in the demonstration they are observing. We rely on five P's as a guide for demonstrating lessons: *Present*, *Practice*, *Participate*, *Ponder*, and *Project*.

First, we lay the foundation for technology integration by *presenting* the potential use of the technology embedded within the context of the lesson. Next, teachers engage in *practice*. In this phase, they rely on our modeling and their existing knowledge to apply what has been observed to the completion of an authentic task (e.g., development of a lesson plan where technology is embedded in the literacy curriculum). Then teachers *participate* in a dialogue about knowledge gained from the experience and the strengths and weaknesses of the selected technology as a support to content-related lessons. This dialogue may be with us, or it may include other teachers if the lesson has been modeled for a group. We then ask teachers to *ponder* their learning in written form. An anecdotal log works well for this purpose. Finally, the reflection process challenges teachers to *project* how they can utilize the featured technology in their future teaching.

Promoting Leadership in the School

Several of the classroom examples presented in this book represent the experiences of teachers in buildings and districts with high levels of administrative support. By this we mean that large sums of money have been allocated to providing the resources necessary to support teachers in their technology integration. In these schools and school districts, administrators have understood that effective technology integration requires much more than hardware, software, and a speedy Internet connection. They have understood and prioritized the importance of supporting teachers' ongoing learning in conjunction with new technologies. Ideally, administrators spend enough time in classrooms and participate with teachers in enough professional development opportunities, to grasp the dynamics of effective literacy–technology integration. Unfortunately, this is not the case in most school settings. According to findings of the Editorial Projects in Education Research Center's 2006 Technology Counts survey, access to technology within schools has expanded far beyond the capacity of school administrators to use technology effectively themselves (Swanson, 2006).

As noted in Chapter 2, the issue of equity as related to technology integration is becoming less and less about disparity in *access* to new technologies than it is about disparity among schools in *use* and *capacity*. An administrative emphasis on technology integration without the development of a plan, a direction, or the support to enhance teacher understanding will not result in the preparation of students who are adept with new technologies and competent in new literacies. Even the most talented teachers and those who are truly committed to meaningful technology integration are severely limited by a lack of effective leadership. Recalling that capacity building and learning to learn are the goals of technology-related professional development, it is essential that building administrators provide increased leadership through their own engagement in these processes.

Promoting Leadership in the District

Having discussed the need to support teachers in the classroom as well as at the building level, it is imperative that we consider the broader context within which teachers and administrators do their daily work with children. In most U.S. schools, the daily work that teachers and administrators do is influenced in large part and in some cases wholly determined by decisions made at the district level. District policy, as well as scheduling and the allocation of financial and human resources, can have a tremendous impact on what teachers can and cannot do in their classrooms. A major challenge facing district-level professional development coordinators and others responsible for large-scale teacher learning efforts is to move beyond traditional approaches to staff development and toward those that are more likely to result in improved student learning via teacher change (Lyons & Pinnell, 2001; Robb, 2000). Robb (2000) describes this move as being from traditional staff development to professional study, with an emphasis on teachers working together over time. She suggests instructional team leaders, peer mentors or coaches, resource teachers, outside consultants, and teacher-organized study groups as ways in which educators can work together to improve instructional practice.

Providing teachers with rich learning opportunities such as these requires a change in the fundamental way in which school districts operate. One example of systemic change is offering continuing education credit for engagement in long-term communities of learning, similarly to the way teachers receive credit for participating in district inservices. In order for teachers to integrate new technologies effectively into their teaching, they need to be supported by the organizations in which they work.

Connecting Communities of Practice

We have found that when teachers come together in a community, there is a ripple effect. They take their professional growth into the other communities in which they hold membership: their classroom, their school, even their communication with parents. For us, the challenge of implementing an innovation in our teacher education courses led the two of us to work together in new ways and to invite others into our learning circle. We often describe our own learning in community with inservice teachers as reciprocal staff development. That is, instead of coming in as "the experts" and participating in a one-way flow of information (from us to the teachers) as is typical of traditional staff development models, we participated in a process of reciprocal professional development, characterized by a flow of information in both directions.

Historically, the communities of preservice teacher educators, inservice teacher professional development facilitators, and classroom teachers have worked independently of one another, despite their shared goal of affecting student learning. We see a future in which these communities operate interdependently to maximize the learning of all teachers and, ultimately, the children who are at the center of the work that we all do. The *intersection* of communities of teacher practice frames our perspective on creating and sustaining teachers who will provide meaningful literacy–technology integration experiences for their students. In the age of learning to learn, there can be no better model for us to move forward as a community of teachers as learners.

FINAL THOUGHTS

In the early days of our work, we were hesitant, even skeptical, about the potential of new technologies to enhance children's literacy learning. Since then, we have learned so much, working alongside teachers such as Leia, Darin, Laura, Jinna, Jon David, and Gail. We have also acquired valuable information and insights from our colleagues who are engaged in cutting-edge research related to new literacies. As we complete this book, it is hard to believe that our work began because of external pressure to integrate technology into the literacy curriculum. Although this book is coming to a close, our journey continues to unfold. What is emerging for us is a change in our attitudes, attributes, and actions related to literacy–technology integration. We trust that this book has challenged you to expand the ways in which you integrate literacy and technology, both today and in the future. With the acceptance of this challenge comes a lasting impact on your students—our technosages of tomorrow.

INQUIRY AND REFLECTION

As a culminating learning opportunity, examine each Inquiry and Reflection activity that you have completed. Select the two that are most meaningful to you. In your anecdotal log, record why they are meaningful and how they will move you forward on your literacy–technology integration journey. Consider sharing these meaningful artifacts representing your ongoing professional development with colleagues and/or an administrator. Return to the first entry in your anecdotal log and examine the goal(s) you recorded regarding literacy–technology integration. Consider the following questions:

> ➤ *Where have you been* on your journey to integrate literacy and technology?

> ➤ *Where are you now* on your journey to integrate literacy and technology?

> ➤ *Where are you going* on your journey to integrate literacy and technology?

A GLOSSARY OF TERMS
New Words Associated with New Technologies

bookmark   The electronic listing of an Internet site for future use. Clicking on the bookmark takes you directly to the site.

browser   A software program that allows you to view pages on the Internet. Examples of browsers are Netscape Navigator, Internet Explorer, and Safari.

homepage   The central page of a website that contains information about the site, including the person or organization who created it, key features, and available links.

hypertext link   Words or icons, often highlighted, that, when clicked, take you directly to related text, image, or sound. A link can take you to an illustration or photograph, a video clip with sound, or another piece of text related to the information presented on a webpage. Links may be updated to reflect the most recent or most important information available. Some of the links found at the website of the National Council of Teachers of English are "About NCTE," "Membership," and "Professional Development."

the Internet   A constellation of computer networks linked worldwide that provides access to e-mail and the World Wide Web.

menu   A list of tools, functions, and features available for use in a software program. Usually, clicking on one item leads to an array of additional choices. Examples of menu items in a word processing program are File, Edit, and Format. Examples of menu items in a browser program are View, History, and Bookmarks.

search engine   A computer program that locates online documents, images, and other files containing words or phrases you specify. Adults commonly use Google and Yahoo! Ask Jeeves for Kids, KidsClick, and Yahooligans! are search engines designed specifically for children.

toolbar   A row of icons, usually appearing at the top of the computer screen, that represent frequently used functions associated with a software program. For instance, icons on the toolbar of a word processing program might allow you to change font size, cut and paste text, or save a document. Toolbars can usually be customized to include the functions you use most often.

URL (Uniform Resource Locator)   The address of a particular location on the Internet. For example, the URL for the International Society for Technology in Education is *www.iste.org.*

World Wide Web   A massive collection of files located on computers around the world that are connected by way of the Internet.

TOOLS FOR THINKING ABOUT TECHNOLOGY INTEGRATION

Appendix A

EXAMINING MY TEACHING ENVIRONMENT FOR CHARACTERISTICS THAT SUPPORT EFFECTIVE LITERACY–TECHNOLOGY INTEGRATION

Characteristics of learning environments that support effective literacy–technology integration	In what ways are these characteristics evident in my teaching situation?	My goal(s) for increasing the presence of these characteristics in my teaching situation.
Integration of conventional and new literacies		
Critical thinking		
Promoting learning to learn		
Integration of literacy instruction with content-area instruction		
Attention to social interaction and collaboration		
Differentiation of instruction		
Equity of access to technology		
Emphasis on the classroom as a learning community		
Multifaceted preparation for instruction coupled with flexibility and responsiveness		
Preservation of fundamental features of exemplary print-based literacy instruction		

WEBSITE REVIEW CHART

Organization and Website Address	Potential Application to My Teaching		
	Planning Instruction	Implementing Instruction	Supporting Professional Development

ORGANIZATIONS THAT SUPPORT STUDENT LEARNING
AND TEACHER PROFESSIONAL DEVELOPMENT

Organizations	Website Addresses (URL)
International Reading Association	*www.reading.org*
National Council for the Social Studies	*www.socialstudies.org*
National Council of Teachers of English	*www.ncte.org*
National Council of Teachers of Mathematics	*www.nctm.org*
International Society for Technology in Education	*www.iste.org*
National Science Teachers Association	*www.nsta.org*
Read Write Think	*ReadWriteThink.org*

GUIDING QUESTIONS FOR WEBQUEST SELECTION

WebQuest review for _____

(name of WebQuest)

Guiding Questions	My Notes
1. Does this WebQuest meet my curriculum goals and learning objectives?	
2. How much time will this take for my students to complete?	
3. Does the WebQuest require my students to think critically about information and evaluate the information they encounter?	
4. Has this WebQuest been developed to accommodate individual learning needs and interests?	
5. Is there an opportunity for students to share the results of their WebQuest with the rest of the class for discussion and additional learning?	
6. Do students know, in advance, how their work on a WebQuest will be evaluated?	
7. Are all of the links in the WebQuest active and appropriate for my students?	

Circle appropriate response:

____ Based on my notes above, I **will** use this WebQuest.

____ Based on my notes above, I **will not** use this WebQuest.

Appendix E

LESSON OBSERVATION GUIDE

Teacher: _____ Observation conducted by: _____

School: _____ Grade: _____ Date: _____

Lesson plan provided? _____ Lesson focus: _____

Literacy–Technology Content Knowledge and Skills

Provide a brief narrative of what is being observed.

Specifically, how is technology being integrated into the curriculum?

Learning Environment

Provide a brief narrative of the learning environment.

Consider the following aspects.

1. Does the teacher provide equitable access to technology tools? Describe.

2. Does the teacher encourage student self-sufficiency and control with technology? Describe.

(continued)

3. Does the teacher effectively manage technology-related equipment and materials? Describe.

4. Does the teacher model expected procedures for students? Describe.

5. Does the teacher effectively manage student groups as they use technology? Describe.

6. Does the teacher effectively meet the needs of diverse learners? Describe.

Appendix F

WORK SAMPLE LABEL

Teacher name: _____ Date taught: _____

Student name: _____

Lesson description: _____

_____

_____

Comments: _____

_____

_____

_____

Appendix G

INSTRUCTIONAL PLANNING GRID

Name: _____   Date: _____

Month	Student Objectives	Preparation	Technology Applications	Evidence of Learning: To what degree have objectives been met for observed students?	Future instructional plans for observed students

PERFORMANCE INDICATORS FOR TECHNOLOGY-LITERATE STUDENTS: PRE-K TO GRADE 2

1. Use input devices (e.g., mouse, keyboard, remote control) and output devices (e.g., monitor, printer) to successfully operate computers, VCRs, audiotapes, and other technologies.

2. Use a variety of media and technology resources for directed and independent learning activities.

3. Communicate about technology using developmentally appropriate and accurate terminology.

4. Use developmentally appropriate multimedia resources (e.g., interactive books, educational software, elementary multimedia encyclopedias) to support learning.

5. Work cooperatively and collaboratively with peers, family members, and others when using technology in the classroom.

6. Demonstrate positive social and ethical behaviors when using technology.

7. Practice responsible use of technology systems and software.

8. Create developmentally appropriate multimedia products with support from teachers, family members, or student partners.

9. Use technology resources (e.g., puzzles, logical thinking programs, writing tools, digital cameras, drawing tools) for problem solving, communication, and illustration of thoughts, ideas, and stories.

10. Gather information and communicate with others using telecommunications, with support from teachers, family members, or student partners.

PERFORMANCE INDICATORS FOR TECHNOLOGY-LITERATE STUDENTS: GRADES 3 TO 5

1. Use keyboards and other common input and output devices (including adaptive devices when necessary) efficiently and effectively.

2. Discuss common uses of technology in daily life and the advantages and disadvantages those uses provide.

3. Discuss basic issues related to responsible use of technology and information and describe personal consequences of inappropriate use.

4. Use general-purpose productivity tools and peripherals to support personal productivity, remediate skill deficits, and facilitate learning throughout the curriculum.

5. Use technology tools (e.g., multimedia authoring, presentation, Web tools, digital cameras, scanners) for individual and collaborative writing, communication, and publishing activities to create knowledge products for audiences inside and outside the classroom.

6. Use telecommunications efficiently to access remote information, communicate with others in support of direct and independent learning, and pursue personal interests.

7. Use telecommunications and online resources (e.g., e-mail, online discussions, Web environments) to participate in collaborative problem-solving activities for the purpose of developing solutions or products for audiences inside and outside the classroom.

8. Use technology resources (e.g., calculators, data collection probes, videos, educational software) for problem solving, self-directed learning, and extended learning activities.

9. Determine which technology is useful and select the appropriate tool(s) and technology resources to address a variety of tasks and problems.

10. Evaluate the accuracy, relevance, appropriateness, comprehensiveness, and bias of electronic information sources.

FAMILY SURVEY OF CHILDREN'S ATTITUDES TOWARD READING, WRITING, AND TECHNOLOGY (COMPLETED BY PARENT/GUARDIAN)

Child's name: _____

What adjectives would you use to describe your child?

What does your child enjoy doing for fun?

What school activities/subjects are most enjoyable for your child?

At this point in the school year, how would you characterize your child's attitude toward reading?

(continued)

At this point in the school year, how would you characterize your child's attitude toward writing?

At this point in the year, how would you characterize your child's attitude toward using the computer?

Does your child use a computer outside of school?

> If so, how often?

> For what purposes?

What else would you like us to know about your child?

CHART FOR REFLECTING ON COMPREHENSION STRATEGY
INSTRUCTION IN MY CLASSROOM

Strategy	How I Teach This Strategy	When I Teach This Strategy
• Setting Purposes for Reading		
• Asking and Answering Questions		
• Examining Text Structure		
• Making Predictions		
• Making Inferences		
• Integrating New Ideas with Prior Knowledge		
• Creating Images and Visual Representations		

(continued)

Strategy	How I Teach This Strategy	When I Teach This Strategy
• Determining What Is Important		
• Skimming, Scanning, and Selective Reading		
• Summarizing and Synthesizing		
• Dealing with Graphic Information		
• Monitoring and Repairing Comprehension		
• Interpreting and Evaluating Information		
• Navigating Text		

REFERENCES

Ahlness, M. (2005). Giving it away: The Earth Day groceries project. In R. A. Karchmer, M. H. Mallette, J. Kara-Soteriou, & D. J. Leu, Jr. (Eds.), *Innovative approaches to literacy education: Using the Internet to support new literacies* (pp. 28–43). Newark, DE: International Reading Association.

Allington, R. L., & Johnston, P. H. (2002). *Reading to learn: Lessons from exemplary fourth-grade classrooms.* New York: Guilford Press.

Allington, R. L., & Walmsley, S. A. (Eds.). (1995). *No quick fix: Rethinking literacy programs in America's elementary schools.* New York: Teachers College Press.

Anderson, R. C. (1996). Research foundations to support wide reading. In V. Greaney (Ed.), *Promoting reading in developing countries* (pp. 55–77). Newark, DE: International Reading Association.

Atkin, J. M., Black, P., & Coffey, J. (2001). *Classroom assessment and the National Science Education Standards.* Washington, DC: National Academy Press.

Au, K. H. (2002). Multicultural factors and the effective instruction of students of diverse backgrounds. In A. E. Farstrup & S. J. Samuels (Eds.), *What research has to say about reading instruction* (3rd ed., pp. 392–413). Newark, DE: International Reading Association.

Au, K. H., & Raphael, T. E. (1998). Curriculum and teaching in literature-based programs. In T. E. Raphael & K. H. Au (Eds.), *Literature-based instruction: Reshaping the curriculum* (pp. 123–148). Norwood, MA: Christopher-Gordon.

Ball, D. L., & Cohen, D. K. (1999). Developing practice, developing practitioners: Toward a practice-based theory of professional education. In L. Darling-Hammond & G. Sykes (Eds.), *Teaching as the learning profession: Handbook of policy and practice* (pp. 3–32). San Francisco: Jossey-Bass.

Beck, I. L., McKeown, M. G., & Kucan, L. (2002). *Bringing words to life: Robust vocabulary instruction.* New York: Guilford Press.

Becker, H. J., Ravitz, J. L., & Wong, Y. T. (1999). Teacher and teacher-directed student use of computers and software. Irvine, CA: Center for Research on Information Technology and Organizations. Retrieved September 26, 2005, from *www.crito. uci.edu/tlc/findings/computeruse/*

Black, P., & Wiliam, D. (1998). Inside the black box: Raising standards through classroom assessment. *Phi Delta Kappan, 80*(2), 139–148.

Borko, H., Davinroy, K. H., Bliem, C. L., & Cumbo, K. B. (2000). Exploring and supporting teacher change: Two third-grade teachers' experiences in a mathematics and literacy staff development project. *Elementary School Journal, 100,* 273–306.

Castek, J., & Bevans-Mangleson, J., & Goldstone, B. (2006). Reading adventures online: Five ways to introduce the new literacies of the Internet through children's literature. *The Reading Teacher, 59* 714–728.

CEO Forum on Education and Technology. (1999). Professional development: A link to better learning. Retrieved November 11, 2002, from *www.ceoforum.org/reports. cfm?RID=2*

Chappuis, J. (2005). Helping students understand assessment. *Educational Leadership, 63*(3), 39–43.

Clarke, J., & Agne, R. (1997). *Interdisciplinary high school teaching.* Needham, MA: Allyn & Bacon.

Coiro, J. (2003). Reading comprehension on the Internet: Expanding our understanding of reading comprehension to encompass new literacies. *The Reading Teacher, 56,* 458–464.

Coiro, J. L. (2005a). Every teacher a Miss Rumphius: Empowering teachers with effective professional development. In R. A. Karchmer, M. H. Mallette, J. Kara-Soteriou, & D. J. Leu, Jr. (Eds.), *Innovative approaches to literacy education: Using the Internet to support new literacies* (pp. 199–219). Newark, DE: International Reading Association.

Coiro, J. (2005b). Making sense of online text. *Educational Leadership, 63,* 30–35.

Coiro, J. (2005c, May). *Reading the Internet: Challenges and possibilities for all readers.* Paper presented at the annual conference of the International Reading Association, San Antonio, TX.

Commeyras, M., & DeGroff, L. (1998). Literacy professionals' perspectives on professional development and pedagogy: A United States survey. *Reading Research Quarterly, 33,* 434–472.

Cuban, L. (2001). *Oversold and underused: Computers in the classroom.* Cambridge, MA: Harvard University Press.

Culp, K. M., Honey, M., & Mandinach, E. (2003). *A retrospective on twenty years of education technology policy.* Washington, DC: U.S. Department of Education.

Danielson, C. (1996). *Enhancing professional practice: A framework for teaching.* Alexandria, VA: Association for Supervision and Curriculum Development.

Day, J. P. (2001). How I became an exemplary teacher (although I'm really still learning just like anyone else). In M. Pressley, R. L. Allington, R. Wharton-McDonald, C. C. Block, & L. M. Morrow, *Learning to read: Lessons from exemplary first-grade classrooms* (pp. 205–218). New York: Guilford Press.

Duke, N. K. (2000). 3.6 minutes per day: The scarcity of informational text in first grade. *Reading Research Quarterly, 35,* 202–224.

Duke, N. K., & Pearson, P. D. (2002). Effective practices for developing reading comprehension. In A. E. Farstrup & S. J. Samuels (Eds.), *What research has to say about reading instruction* (3rd ed., pp. 205–242). Newark, DE: International Reading Association.

Durkin, D. (2004). *Teaching them to read* (6th ed.). Boston: Allyn & Bacon.

Edwards, P. A., Pleasants, H. M., & Franklin, S. H. (1999). *A path to follow: Learning to listen to parents.* Portsmouth, NH: Heinemann.

Encarta® World English Dictionary [Computer software]. (1999). Redmond, WA: Microsoft Corporation.

Fawcett, G., & Snyder, S. (1998). Transforming schools through systemic change: New work, new knowledge, new technology. In D. Reinking, M. C. McKenna, L. D. Labbo, & R. D. Kieffer (Eds.), *Handbook of literacy and technology: Transformation in a post-typographic world* (pp. 115–127). Mahwah, NJ: Erlbaum.

Fisher, D., Lapp, D., & Flood, J. (2000). How is technology really used for literacy instruction in elementary and middle school classrooms? *National Reading Conference Yearbook, 49,* 464–476.

Fullen, M. (2001). *The new meaning of educational change* (3rd ed.). New York: Teachers College Press.

Gambrell, L. B., & Mazzoni, S. A. (1999). Principles of best practice: Finding the common ground. In L. B. Gambrell, L. M. Morrow, S. B. Neuman, & M. Pressley (Eds.), *Best practices in literacy instruction* (pp. 11–21). New York: Guilford Press.

Gambrell, L. B., Morrow, L. M., Neuman, S. B., & Pressley, M. (Eds.). (1999). *Best practices in literacy instruction.* New York: Guilford Press.

Graves, M. F., Juel, C., & Graves, B. B. (2004). *Teaching reading in the 21st century* (3rd ed.). Boston: Allyn & Bacon.

Gunning, T. G. (2003). *Creating literacy instruction for all children* (4th ed.). Boston: Allyn & Bacon.

Guthrie, J. T., & Wigfield, A. (2000). Engagement and motivation in reading. In M. L. Kamil, P. B. Mosenthal, P. D. Pearson, & R. Barr (Eds.), *Handbook of reading research* (Vol. 3, pp. 403–422). Mahwah, NJ: Erlbaum.

Harris, T. L., & Hodges, R. E. (Eds.). (1995). *The literacy dictionary: The vocabulary of reading and writing.* Newark, DE: International Reading Association.

Heacox, D. (2002). Differentiating instruction in the regular classroom: How to reach and teach all learners, grades 3–12. Minneapolis, MN: Free Spirit Publishing.

Hubert, D. (2005). The Flat Stanley Project and other authentic applications of technology in the classroom. In R. A. Karchmer, M. H. Mallette, J. Kara-Soteriou, & D. J. Leu, Jr. (Eds.), *Innovative approaches to literacy education: Using the Internet to support new literacies* (pp. 121–137). Newark, DE: International Reading Association.

International Reading Association. (2000). *Making a difference means making it different: Honoring children's rights to excellent reading instruction.* Newark, DE: International Reading Association.

International Reading Association. (2002). *Integrating literacy and technology in the curriculum* [Brochure]. Newark, DE: International Reading Association.

International Society for Technology in Education. (2000). *National educational technology standards for teachers: Connecting curriculum and technology.* Washington,

DC: Author. Retrieved September 26, 2005, from *www.iste.org/inhouse/nets/cnets/teachers/t_stands.html*

Johnson, D. (2005). Miss Rumphius as a role model for preservice teachers. In R. A. Karchmer, M. H. Mallette, J. Kara-Soteriou, & D. J. Leu, Jr. (Eds.), *Innovative approaches to literacy education: Using the Internet to support new literacies* (pp. 182–198). Newark, DE: International Reading Association.

Johnson, D. W., & Johnson, R. T. (2004). Cooperation and the use of technology. In D. H. Jonassen (Ed.), *Handbook of research for educational communications and technology* (2nd ed., pp. 785–811). Mahwah, NJ: Erlbaum.

Johnson, D. W., Johnson, R. T., & Holubec, E. J. (1991). *Cooperation in the classroom* (5th ed.). Edina, MN: Interaction Book Company.

Kamil, M. L., Intrator, S. M., & Kim, H. S. (2000). The effects of other technologies on literacy and literacy learning. In M. L. Kamil, P. B. Mosenthal, P. D. Pearson, & R. Barr (Eds.), *Handbook of reading research* (Vol. 3, pp. 771–788). Mahwah, NJ: Erlbaum.

Karchmer, R. A. (2001). The journey ahead: Thirteen teachers report how the Internet influences literacy and literacy instruction in their K–12 classrooms. *Reading Research Quarterly, 36,* 442–466.

Karchmer, R. A., Mallette, M. H., Kara-Soteriou, J., & Leu, D. J., Jr. (Eds.). (2005). *Innovative approaches to literacy education: Using the Internet to support new literacies.* Newark, DE: International Reading Association.

Kist, W. (2005). *New literacies in action: Teaching and learning in multiple media.* New York: Teachers College Press.

Kucan, L., & Beck, I. L. (1997). Thinking aloud and reading comprehension research: Inquiry, instruction, and social interaction. *Review of Educational Research, 67,* 271–299.

Kymes, A. (2005). Teaching online comprehension strategies using think-alouds. *Journal of Adolescent and Adult Literacy, 48,* 492–500.

Labbo, L. D. (2005a). Fundamental qualities of effective literacy instruction: An exploration of worthwhile classroom practices. In R. A. Karchmer, M. H. Mallette, J. Kara-Soteriou, & D. J. Leu, Jr. (Eds.), *Innovative approaches to literacy education: Using the Internet to support new literacies* (pp. 165–179). Newark, DE: International Reading Association.

Labbo, L. D. (2005b). Professional development in your pajamas? *Language Arts, 82,* 343.

Labbo, L. D., & Kuhn, M. (1998). Electronic symbol making: Young children's computer-related emerging concepts about literacy. In D. Reinking, M. C. McKenna, L. D. Labbo, & R. D. Kieffer (Eds.), *Handbook of literacy and technology: Transformations in a post-typographic world* (pp. 79–91). Mahwah, NJ: Erlbaum.

Labbo, L. D., & Reinking, D. (1999). Negotiating the multiple realities of technology in literacy research and instruction. *Reading Research Quarterly, 34,* 478–492.

Labbo, L. D., Reinking, D., & McKenna, M. C. (1999). The use of technology in literacy programs. In L. B. Gambrell, L. M. Morrow, S. B. Neuman, & M. Pressley (Eds.), *Best practices in literacy instruction* (pp. 311–327). New York: Guilford Press.

Leahy, S., Lyon, C., Thompson, M., & Wiliam, D. (2005). Classroom assessment: Minute by minute, day by day. *Educational Leadership, 63*(3), 19–24.

Leu, D. J., Jr. (2000). Continuously changing technologies and envisionments for literacy: Deictic consequences for literacy education in an information age. In M. Kamil, P. Mosenthal, P. D. Pearson, & R. Barr (Eds.), *Handbook of reading research* (Vol. 3, pp. 743–770). Mahwah, NJ: Erlbaum.

Leu, D. J., Jr., Kinzer, C. G., Coiro, J., & Cammack, D. (2004). Toward a theory of new literacies emerging from the Internet and other information and communication technologies. In R. R. Ruddell & N. J. Unrauh (Eds.), *Theoretical models and processes of reading* (5th ed., pp. 1570–1613). Newark, DE: International Reading Association.

Leu, D. J., Jr., Leu, D. D., & Coiro, J. (2004). *Teaching with the Internet K–12: New literacies for new times* (4th ed.). Norwood, MA: Christopher-Gordon.

Leu, D. J., Jr., Mallette, M. H., Karchmer, R. A., & Kara-Soteriou, J. (2005). Contextualizing the new literacies of information and communication technologies in theory, research, and practice. In R. A. Karchmer, M. H. Mallette, J. Kara-Soteriou, & D. J. Leu, Jr. (Eds.), *Innovative approaches to literacy education: Using the Internet to support new literacies* (pp. 1–10). Newark, DE: International Reading Association.

Lyons, C. A., & Pinnell, G. S. (2001). *Systems for change in literacy education: A guide to professional development*. Portsmouth, NH: Heinemann.

Marzano, R. J. (1992). *A different kind of classroom: Teaching with dimensions of learning*. Alexandria, VA: ASCD.

McGrail, E. (2004, December). *Lids up, lids down: Three teachers grapple with laptop technology in the high school English language arts classroom*. Paper presented at the meeting of the National Reading Conference, San Antonio, TX.

McKenna, M. (1998). Electronic texts and the transformation of beginning reading. In D. Reinking, M. C. McKenna, L. D. Labbo, & R. D. Kieffer (Eds.), *Handbook of literacy and technology: Transformations in a post-typographic world* (pp. 45–59). Mahwah, NJ: Erlbaum.

McKenna, M. C., Labbo, L. D., & Reinking D. (2003). Effective use of technology in literacy instruction. In L. M. Morrow, L. B. Gambrell, & M. Pressley (Eds.), *Best practices in literacy instruction* (2nd ed., pp. 307–331). New York: Guilford Press.

McTighe, J., & O'Connor, K. (2005). Seven practices to effective learning. *Educational Leadership, 63*(3), 10–17.

Milken Exchange on Education Technology and International Society for Technology in Education (1999). *Will new teachers be prepared to teach in a digital age?: A national survey on information technology in teacher education*. Retrieved November 11, 2005, from *www.mff.org/publications/publications.taf?page=154*

Minnesota Department of Education. (2003, May 19). *Standards in language arts K–12*. Retrieved April 18, 2006, from the *www.education.state.mn.us/html/mde_home.htm*

Munroe, B. (2004). *Crossing the digital divide: Race, writing, and technology in the classroom*. New York: Teachers College Press.

National Center for Education Statistics. (2000). *Teachers' tools for the 21st century: A report on teachers' use of technology*. Washington, DC: U.S. Department of Education.

National Council for the Accreditation of Teacher Education. (1997). *Technology and the new professional teacher: Preparing for the 21st-century classroom.* Retrieved July 3, 2002, from the *www.ncate.org/projects/tech*

National Council of Teachers of English and International Reading Association. (1996). *Standards for the English language arts.* Newark, DE: International Reading Association.

National Reading Panel. (2000). *Report of the National Reading Panel: Reports of the subgroups.* Washington, DC: National Institute of Child Health and Human Development Clearinghouse.

No Child Left Behind Act. (2002). Public Law No. 107–110. Retrieved June 12, 2005, from *www.nclb.org*

Norton, P., & Wiburg, K. M. (1998). *Teaching with technology.* Fort Worth, TX: Harcourt Brace College.

Norton, P., & Wiburg, K. M. (2003). *Teaching with technology: Designing opportunities to learn* (2nd ed.). Belmont, CA: Wadsworth/Thomson Learning.

Ogle, D. (1986). K-W-L: A teaching model that develops active reading of expository text. *Reading Teacher, 39,* 564–570.

Palincsar, A. S., & Brown, A. L. (1986). Interactive teaching to promote independent learning from text. *The Reading Teacher, 39,* 771–777.

Pearson, P. D., & Gallagher, M. C. (1983). The instruction of reading comprehension. *Contemporary Educational Psychology, 8,* 317–344.

Pearson, P. D., Roehler, L. R., Dole, J. A., & Duffy, G. G. (1992). Developing expertise in reading comprehension. In S. J. Samuels & A. E. Farstup (Eds.), *What research has to say about reading instruction* (2nd ed, pp. 145–199). Newark, DE: International Reading Association.

Pressley, M. (1998). *Reading instruction that works: The case for balanced teaching.* New York: Guilford Press.

Pressley, M. (2000). What should comprehension instruction be the instruction of? In M. L. Kamil, P. B. Mosenthal, P. D. Pearson, & R. Barr (Eds.), *Handbook of reading research* (Vol. 3, pp. 545–561). Mahwah, NJ: Erlbaum.

Pressley, M. (2002). Metacognition and self-regulated comprehension. In A. E. Farstrup & S. J. Samuels (Eds.), *What research has to say about reading instruction* (3rd ed., pp. 291–309). Newark, DE: International Reading Association.

Pressley, M., & Afflerbach, P. (1995). *Verbal protocols for reading: The nature of constructively responsive reading.* Hillsdale, NJ: Erlbaum.

Pressley, M., Allington, R. L., Wharton-McDonald, R., Block, C. C., & Morrow, L. M. (2001). *Learning to read: Lessons from exemplary first-grade classrooms.* New York: Guilford Press.

Pressley, M., & Block, C. C. (2002). Summing up: What comprehension instruction could be. In C. C. Block & M. Pressley (Eds.), *Comprehension instruction: Research-based best practices* (pp. 383–392). New York: Guilford Press.

Raphael, T. (1982). Question-answering strategies for children. *The Reading Teacher, 36,* 186–190.

Raphael, T., Pardo, L., Highfield, K., & McMahon, S. (1997). *Book Club: A literature-based curriculum.* Littleton, MA: Small Planets Communications, Inc.

Richards, J. (2001). "I did not plan ahead": Preservice teachers' concerns integrating print-based lessons with computer technology. In J. V. Hoffman, D. L. Schallert, C. M. Fairbanks, J. Worthy, & B. Maloch (Eds.), *The 50th yearbook of the National Reading Conference* (pp. 507–518). Chicago: National Reading Conference.

Robb, L. (2000). *Redefining staff development: A collaborative model for teachers and administrators.* Portsmouth, NH: Heinemann.

Sanguiliano, G. (2005). Books on tape for kids: A language arts-based service-learning project. In R. A. Karchmer, M. H. Mallette, J. Kara-Soteriou, & D. J. Leu, Jr. (Eds.), *Innovative approaches to literacy education: Using the Internet to support new literacies* (pp. 13–27). Newark, DE: International Reading Association.

Schmar-Dobler, E. (2003). Reading on the Internet: The link between literacy and technology. *Journal of Adolescent and Adult Literacy, 47,* 80–85.

Scott, J. A. (2004). Scaffolding vocabulary learning: Ideas for equity in urban settings. In D. Lapp, C. C. Block, E. J. Cooper, J. Flood, N. Roser, & J. V. Tinajero (Eds.), *Teaching all the children: Strategies for developing literacy in an urban setting* (pp. 275–293). New York: Guilford Press.

Senge, P. M. (1990). *The fifth discipline.* New York: Doubleday.

Sheingold, K., & Frederiksen, J. (2000). Using technology to support innovative assessment. *The Jossey-Bass Reader on: Technology and learning* (pp. 320–337). San Francisco: Jossey-Bass.

Shockley, B., Michalove, B., & Allen, J. (1995). *Engaging families: Connecting home and school literacy communities.* Portsmouth, NH: Heinemann.

Short, K. G., Schroeder, J., Laird, J., Kauffman, G., Ferguson, M. J., & Crawford, K. M. (1996). *Learning together through inquiry: From Columbus to integrated curriculum.* York, ME: Stenhouse.

Stiggins, R. J., Arter, J., Chappuis, J., & Chappuis, S. (2004). *Classroom assessment for student learning: Doing it right—using it well.* Portland, OR: Assessment Training Institute.

Swanson, C. B. (2006). Technology counts '06: Tracking U.S. trends. Retrieved May 18, 2006, from *www.edweek.org/ew/articles/2006/05/04/35trends.h25.html?levelId=1000*

Sykes, G. (1999). Teacher and student learning: Strengthening their connection. In L. Darling-Hammond & G. Sykes (Eds.), *Teaching as the learning profession: Handbook of policy and practice* (pp. 151–179). San Francisco: Jossey-Bass.

Tapscott, D. (1998). *Growing up digital: The rise of the Net generation.* New York: McGraw-Hill.

Taylor, B. M., Harris, L. A., Pearson, P. D., Garcia, G. (1998). *Reading difficulties: Instruction and assessment* (2nd ed.). New York: McGraw-Hill.

Taylor, B. M., & Pearson, P. D. (2002). *Teaching reading: Effective schools, accomplished teachers.* Mahwah, NJ: Erlbaum.

Thomas, M., & King, A. (2006, May). *The Tablet PC: Old and new literacy in one device.* Paper presented at the annual conference of the International Reading Association, Chicago.

Tomlinson, C. A. (2003). *Fulfilling the promise of the differentiated classroom: Strategies and tools for responsive teaching.* Alexandria, VA: Association for Supervision and Curriculum Development.

Valmont, W. J. (2003). *Technology for literacy teaching and learning.* Boston: Houghton Mifflin.

Vygotsky, L. S. (1978). *Mind in society*. Cambridge, MA: Harvard University Press.

Watts-Taffe, S., & Gwinn, C. G. (2005). Viewing professional development through the lens of technology integration: How do beginning teachers navigate the use of technology and new literacies? In B. Maloch, J. V. Hoffman, D. Schallert, C. M. Fairbanks, & J. Worthy (Eds.), *The 54th yearbook of the National Reading Conference* (pp. 443–454). Oak Creek, WI: National Reading Conference.

Watts-Taffe, S., Gwinn, C. B., Johnson, J. R., & Horn, M. L. (2003). Preparing preservice teachers to integrate technology into the elementary literacy program. *The Reading Teacher, 57,* 130–138.

Wenglinski, H. (2005). *Using technology wisely: The keys to success in schools*. New York: Teachers College Press.

Wepner, S. B., & Ray, L. C. (2000). Using technology for reading development. In S. B. Wepner, W. J. Valmont, & R. Thurlow (Eds.), *Linking literacy and technology: A guide for K–8 classrooms* (pp. 76–105). Newark, DE: International Reading Association.

Wepner, S. B., & Tao, L. (2002). From master teacher to master novice: Shifting responsibilities in technology-infused classrooms. *The Reading Teacher, 55,* 642–651.

Worthy, J., Broaddus, K., & Ivey, G. (2001). *Pathways to independence: Reading, writing, and learning in grades 3–8*. New York: Guilford Press.

Worthy, J., & Roser, N. (2004). Flood ensurance: When children have books they can and want to read. In D. Lapp, C. C. Block, E. J. Cooper, J. Flood, N. Roser, & J. V. Tinajero (Eds.), *Teaching all the children: Strategies for developing literacy in an urban setting* (pp. 179–192). New York: Guilford Press.

Zeichner, K. M., & Liston, D. P. (1996). *Reflective teaching: An introduction*. Mahwah, NJ: Erlbaum.

CHILDREN'S LITERATURE

Atwater, R., & Atwater, F. (1938). *Mr. Popper's penguins*. New York: Dell.

Barrett, J. (1978). *Cloudy with a chance of meatballs*. New York: Simon & Schuster.

Brown, J., & Bjorkman, S. (1964). *Flat Stanley*. New York: HarperCollins.

DiCamillo, K. (2000). *Because of Winn-Dixie*. Cambridge, MA: Candlewick Press.

Hollyer, B. (1999). *Wake up, world!: A day in the life of children around the world*. New York: Henry Holt in association with Oxfam.

Rawls, W. (1961). *Where the red fern grows*. New York: Dell Laurel-Leaf.

Naylor, P. R. (1991). *Shiloh*. New York: Atheneum.

Taylor, M. (1976). *Roll of thunder, hear my cry*. New York: Dial.

INDEX

Page numbers followed by *f* indicate figure

Action plans, 57
Anecdotal log, 10, 38
Assessment
    'approaches to, 78–83
    in decision making, 76–90
    as development, 78
    diagnostic, 78
    formative, 78
    as inquiry, 78
    instruction guided by, 88
    in instructional cycle, 85–88
    involving students in, 83–85
    of learning, 34, 37–38
    of literacy instruction, 34–35, 35*f*, 38
    as measurement of progress, 78
    planning informed by, 87–88
    purposes of, 78–85
    quality control versus quality assurance in, 85–86
    questions in, 84–85, 85*f*, 89–90
    self, by students, 84–85, 86*f*
    summative, 78
    technology in, 89
Attitude
    children's, family survey of, 131–132
    teacher, 96–97

Capacity building, 29–30
CD-ROM, encyclopedia on, 44
Change agents
    actions of, 97–98
    attitudes of, 96–97
    characteristics of, 93–99
    as decision makers, 93–94
    exploration by, 98
    functions of, 92–93
    persistence of, 98
    personal professional development and, 99–100

reflection by, 100–101
    self-efficacy of, 94–95
    vision of, 95–96
ClarisWorks for Kids, 14
Classroom. *See also* specific grade levels
    ICTs and, 3
    as learning community, 19–20, 73–74
    promoting leadership in, 113
Coaches, students as, 56
Coaching, instructional, 113
Collaboration
    attention to, 16–17
    engaging in, 108–109
    teacher, 97–98
Communication
    with colleagues, 97–98, 108–109
    with parents, 48–49
Communication competencies for digital age
    class newspapers and, 69–73
    instructional approaches to, 71
    technological innovation and, 71–73
    writing/writing process and, 70–71
Community
    creating, 19–20, 73–74, 111–112, 115
    professional development, 39–42, 41*f*
Comprehension
    monitoring/repairing, 63
    teaching in kindergarten, 64
Comprehension instruction
    chart for reflecting on, 133–134
    five-step model of, 66
    for reading in digital age, 61–64, 64*f*
Computers
    access to, 18–19
    learning about, 107–108
    See also Information and communications
        technologies

Constructivist approach, 22
Critical thinking, 14–15, 35
Curriculum, designing, 107

Debriefing, follow-up, 37
Decision making
  assessment and, 76–90
  teachers' role in, 93–94
Demonstration, interactive, 26–27
Digital divide, 18. *See also* Information and
  communications technologies, equal access to

E-mail, communication with, 72–73
Earth Day Groceries project, 95
Educational software, 52–53, 52f, 53f
Electronic text, reading, in first grade, 58–59
Encyclopedia, on CD-ROM, 44

Family Survey of Children's Attitudes toward Reading,
  Writing, and Technology, 48–49
Fifth-grade classroom
  creating newspapers in, 69–73
  technology in support of content-area literacy
    in, 76–77
First-grade classroom, reading electronic text in, 58–59
Five P's, 113
Focus groups, 41, 41f
Fourth-grade classroom, creating newspapers in, 69–73

Goals, instructional, 12, 13f, 14, 15f
Golden Book Encyclopedia
  on CD-ROM, 54–55
  software for, 52–54
Graphic information, dealing with, 63

Home–school partnerships, 19
Human resources, 50, 54, 55–56, 108

ICTs. *See* Information and communications
  technologies
Images, creating, 62
Inferences, 62
Information
  evaluating, 55, 64f, 65
  Internet searches for, 59
  interpreting and evaluating, 63
Information and communications technologies
  as agents of change, 102–103
  characteristics of, 3–4
  equal access to, 18–19, 96, 114
  impacts of, 2–3
  learning maximization with, 17–18
  principles of, 3
Instruction. *See* Literacy instruction
Instructional coaching, 113
Instructional cycle
  assessment in, 85–88
  phases of, 30–31, 30f
    connecting, 38–42
  in second-grade classroom, 31–35, 35f
  technology in, 30–35
Instructional goals, 12, 13f, 14, 15f
Instructional objectives, 45–49
Instructional observations, 37, 37f

Instructional preparation, multifaceted, 20
Interactive demonstration, 26–27
Interest inventories, 79, 80f
International Reading Association
  online resources of, 50
  standards of, 45, 46f, 47
  website for, 36, 123
International Society for Technology in Education, 1
  comparison of traditional versus new learning
    environments, 22, 22f
  competency areas of, 101, 102f
  performance indicators of, 45
  website for, 13, 123
Internet
  and approaches to reading comprehension, 68–69
  appropriate use policies for, 36
  equal access to, 18–19, 96, 114
  evaluating information from, 64f, 65
  information searches on, 60
  multicultural worldview and, 19–20
  "reading," 60–61, 61f
  reading skills needed for, 59
  reading/researching, in third-grade class, 65–68
  resources on, 50, 51f, 52
  student resources on, 54–55
  synthesizing sources from, 72f
  teacher resources on, 101
  and teaching reading comprehension, 68–69
Interviews, process, 81–82
ISTE. *See* International Society for Technology in
  Education

Kindergarten, comprehension instruction in, 64

Leadership
  in classroom, 113
  in district, 114–115
  in school, 114
  See also Change agents
Learning
  assessing, 34, 37–38
  practices for, 79, 79f
  promoting, 15–16
  websites supporting, 123
Learning community, creating, 19–20
Learning environments, 11–28
  characteristics of, 13–20
  critical thinking in, 14–15
  equal access to, 18–19, 96
  evaluation form for, 121
  differentiation of instruction, 17–18
  integrating literacy instruction with content-area
    instruction in, 16
  integration of conventional–new literacies in, 14
  motivation and engagement in, 21
  multifaceted instructional preparation in, 20
  new
    envisioning, 22–28
    National Educational Technology Standards for
      Students and, 22, 22f
    versus traditional, 22, 22f
  promoting learning to learn in, 15–16
  social interaction and collaboration in, 16–17
Learning standards, 45, 46f, 47

Lessons, demonstrating, with five P's, 113
Literacy(ies)
    connecting with content-area instruction, 74
    content-area, technology in support of, 76–77
    home–school partnership and, 19
    for Internet, 59
    new
        characteristics of, 4
        defining, 4
        integration with conventional literacy, 14
    paper-and-pencil. See Paper-and-pencil literacy
    performance indicators for, 129–130
    technological innovation and, 2
    traditional, 4
    websites on, 36
Literacy instruction
    age-appropriate, 64
    approaches to, 22–27, 65–68, 71
    assessing and reflecting on, 34–35, 35f, 38
    assessment-guided, 88
    best practices for, 73–75
    differentiation of, 17–18
    integrating with content-area instruction, 16
    meaningful, purpose-driven, 33–34, 37
    multifaceted preparation for, 20
    print-based features in, 20, 21f
    teacher explicit, 24
    teacher preparation for, 44–45
Literacy–technology integration
    anecdotal log of, 10
    collaboration and communication in, 108–109
    current and future aspects of, 3
    decision making about, 8
    determining what and how to teach, 107
Literacy–technology integration (cont.)
    as dimension of change, 102–103
    early years of, 106–110
    effective teaching with, 8
    future of, 112–115
    human resources in, 108
    learning environment for, 8
    nature of, 2–5
    navigating tools and logistics of, 107–108
    need for, 1
    planning for. See Planning
    promoting learning to learn in, 109–110
    questions about, 1–2
    reflection and self-assessment in, 109
    surprises encountered in, 110–112
    teacher as change agent in, 8
    teacher development for, 5–7
    teacher impacts of, 8
    teacher learning opportunities in, 8
    and teacher learning transparency, 110
    teacher's guide to, 29–42
    teaching in context of, 4–5

Miss Rumphius Award, 95, 105
Modeling, 24, 26, 64, 67
Motivation, 21, 110–111

National Council for the Accreditation of Teacher
        Education, standards of, 107
National Council for the Social Studies, website for, 123

National Council of Teachers of English
    online resources of, 50
    standards of, 45, 46f, 47
    website for, 123
National Council of Teachers of Mathematics, website
        for, 123
National Educational Technology Standards for
        Students, 1, 12, 13, 13f, 47
    new learning environments and, 22, 22f
National Educational Technology Standards for
        Teachers, changes in, 101
National Science Teachers Association, website for,
        123
Newspapers, for teaching communication
        competencies, 69–73
No Child Left Behind Act of 2002, 45, 107

Observations
    guide for, 125–126
    instructional, 37, 37f
    teacher, 79, 81

Paper-and-pencil literacy, 12
    preserving features of, 20, 21f
Parents, communicating with, 48–49
Planning, 8, 32–33, 36
    action plans in, 57
    assessment's role in, 87–88
    and capitalizing on student strengths, 47–49
    grid for, 128
    instructional objectives in, 45–49
    learning standards in, 45–49
    resources for, 49–57
        for students, 54–57
        for teachers, 49–54
    in second-grade classroom, 43–57
Planning grids, 38–39, 39f, 40f
Portfolios, 82–83
PowerPoint, 71
Process interviews, 81–82
Professional development, 99–100
    organizations supporting, 123

Questions
    asking and answering, 62
    in assessment, 84–85, 85f
    for WebQuest, 124

Reading
    selective, 63
    setting purposes for, 62
Reading competencies for digital age, 60–69
    comprehension strategies in, 61–64, 64f
    instructional approaches to, 65–68
Reading comprehension
    Internet opportunities for, 68–69
    teaching strategies for
        describing, 66–67
        independent use of, 68
        modeling, 67
        practicing, 67
        using with gradual release of responsibility,
            67
ReadWriteThink, website for, 50, 51f, 123

Reflection
    engaging in, 109
    importance of, 100–101
    role of, 84, 89–90
Research, traditional/new strategies for, 44–47
Resources
    human, 50, 54, 55–56
    planning, 49–57
    students as, 56
    supporting materials as, 56–57
Responsibility, gradual release of, 22–23
RTEACHER listserv, 50

Scaffolding, 22–24
Scanning, 63
School district, resources of, 49–50
Schools, promoting leadership in, 113
Science Education Content Standards, 47
Second-grade classroom
    instructional cycle in, 31–35, 35f
    planning in, 43–57
Self-assessment, engaging in, 109
Self-efficacy, 94–95
Self-motivation, 110–111
Skimming, 63
Social interaction, attention to, 16–17
Software
    educational, 52–53, 52f, 53f
    learning about, 107–108
    literacy development and, 73
    newspaper creation and, 71–72
Student portfolios, 82–83
Students
    emphasizing strengths of, 47–49
    fostering growth of, 84
    individual needs of, 66, 74–75
    motivation and engagement of, 21
    as procedural coaches, 56
    as resources, 56
    resources for, 54–57
        human, 55–57
        online, 54–55
    self-assessment form for, 86f
    teaching how to evaluate information, 55, 65
    zone of development of, 23
Summarizing, 63
Synthesizing, 63

Teacher explicit instruction, 24
Teacher modeling, 24, 26
Teachers
    as change agents, 28, 91–104. See also Change
        agents
    changing role of, 101–102, 102f
    as decision makers, 75
    learning opportunities for, 35–42
    learning, transparency of, 110
    observations by, 79, 81
    preparation for literacy–technology integration, 5–7
    preparation of, 44, 112
    resources for
        in building/district, 49–50
        educational software, 52–53, 52f, 53f
        human, 54
        online, 50, 51f, 52
    self-assessment by, 109
    stories of, 5–7
    support for, 113–115
    technology's impacts on, 105–116
Teaching
    constructivist approach to, 22
    ICTs and, 3–5
    and impacts of technology, 3
    methods of, 23–27
Technology
    in assessment, 89
    effective classroom use of, 58–75
    equal access to, 18–19, 96, 114
    impact on teachers, 105–116
    literacy and, 2
    role in instructional cycle, 30–35
    student motivation and, 21
    in support of content-area literacy, 76–77
    See also Communication competencies for
        digital age; Reading competencies for digital
        age
Texts
    electronic, 65
    examining structure of, 62
    making predictions about, 62
    navigating, 63–64
    Web-based, 60–61, 61f
Think-aloud instruction method, 26, 64
Thinking, critical, 14–15, 35
Third-grade classroom
    creating newspapers in, 69–73
    instructional approaches in, 65–68
"3.6 Minutes Per Day: The Scarcity of Informational
    Text in First Grade" study,
    74
Title I, 48–49

Venn diagram, 82f

Wake Up, World! A Day in the Life of Children Around
    the World, 32–33
Web links, predicting usefulness of, 24, 25f
Webpages, saving, 64
WebQuest, 36
    guiding questions for, 124
Websites
    Four A's for evaluating, 55
    information searches on, 60
    literacy-related, 36
    moving within and among, 63–64
    navigating, 59, 65
    resources on, 50, 51f, 52
    review chart for, 122
    student resources on, 54–55
Word processing, literacy development and, 71–73
Workplace, ICTs and, 3
Writing, teaching with class newspapers, 70–71

Yahooligans!, 55

Zone of development, 23